Phillip K. Trocki

Modern Curriculum Press
Parsippany

EXECUTIVE EDITOR   Wendy Whitnah

PROJECT EDITOR   Diane Dzamtovski

EDITORIAL DEVELOPMENT
DESIGN AND PRODUCTION   The Hampton-Brown Company

ILLUSTRATORS   Anthony Accardo, Joe Boddy, Roberta Collier-Morales, Sandra Forrest, Carlos
Freire, Ron Grauer, Meryl Henderson, Jane McCreary, Yoshi Miyake, Masami
Miyamoto, Deborah Morse, Doug Roy, John Sandford, Rosalind Solomon.

PHOTO CREDITS   25, Comstock; 57, Carlos Valdes-Dapena/Comstock; 60, Thomas Wear/Comstock;
61, Roberta Hershenson/Photo Researchers; 62, Henry Georgi/Comstock;
63, Bob Daemmrich/Uniphoto; 64, Barbara Rios/Photo Researchers;
89, J. Carmichael Jr./Image Bank; 93, J.H. Robinson/Animals Animals;
125, Robert A. Lubeck/Earth Scenes; 133, Sobol/Sipa Press;
141, John P. Kelly/Image Bank.

COVER DESIGN   The Hampton-Brown Company
COVER PHOTO   Steve Satushek/Image Bank

Typefaces for the manuscript type in this book were provided
by Zaner-Bloser, Inc., Columbus, Ohio, copyright, 1993.

Copyright © 1994 by Modern Curriculum Press, Inc.

Modern Curriculum Press

An imprint of Pearson Learning
299 Jefferson Road, P.O. Box 480
Parsippany, NJ 07054–0480

www.pearsonlearning.com

ISBN 0-8136-2840-7

14   05

Table of Contents

Spelling Workout—Our Philosophy

Integration of Spelling with Reading and Writing

In each core lesson for *Spelling Workout,* students read spelling words in context in a variety of expository selections and genre, including poetry, riddles, and stories. The reading selections provide opportunities for reading across the curriculum, focusing on the subject areas of science, social studies, health, and language arts.

After students read the selection and practice writing their spelling words, they use List Words to help them write about a related topic in a variety of forms and innovations such as poems, letters, recipes, descriptions, jokes, and signs.

The study of spelling should not be limited to a specific time in the school day. Use opportunities throughout the day to reinforce and maintain spelling skills by integrating spelling with other curriculum areas. Point out spelling words in books, texts, and the student's own writing. Encourage students to write, as they practice spelling through writing. Provide opportunities for writing with a purpose.

Phonics-Based Instructional Design

Spelling Workout takes a solid phonic and structural analysis approach to encoding. The close tie between spelling and phonics allows each to reinforce the other. *Spelling Workout* correlates closely to *MCP Phonics, MCP Discovery Phonics I* and *II,* and other phonics material published by Modern Curriculum Press, although these programs are complete within themselves and can be used independently. In addition, lessons are correlated to the phonics strategies in Silver Burdett Ginn *New Dimensions in the World of Reading* Teacher's Editions.

Research-Based Teaching Strategies

Spelling Workout utilizes a test-study-test method of teaching spelling. The student first takes a pretest of words that have not yet been introduced. Under the direction of the teacher, the student then self-corrects the test, rewriting correctly any word that has been missed. This approach not only provides an opportunity to determine how many words a student can already spell but also allows students to analyze spelling mistakes. In the process students also discover patterns that make it easier to spell List Words. Students study the words as they work through practice exercises, and then reassess their spelling by taking a final test.

High-Utility List Words

The words used in *Spelling Workout* have been chosen for their frequency in students' written and oral vocabularies, their relationships to subject areas, and for structural as well as phonetic generalizations. Each List Word has been cross-referenced with one or more of the following:

Carroll, Davies, and Richman. *The American Heritage Word Frequency Book*

Dale and O'Rourke. *The Living Word Vocabulary*

Dolch. *220 Basic Sight Words*

Fry, Polk, and Fountoukidis. "Spelling Demons—197 Words Frequently Misspelled by Elementary Students"

Green and Loomer. *The New Iowa Spelling Scale*

Harris and Jacobson. *Basic Elementary Reading Vocabularies*

Hanna. *Phoneme Grapheme Correspondences as Cues to Spelling Improvement*

Hillerich. *A Written Vocabulary of Elementary Children*

Kucera and Francis. *Computational Analysis of Present-Day American English*

Rinsland. *A Basic Vocabulary of Elementary Children*

Sakiey and Fry. *3000 Instant Words*

Thomas. "3000 Words Most Frequently Written"

Thomas. "200 Words Most Frequently Misspelled"

A Format That Results in Success

Spelling Workout treats spelling as a developmental process. Students progress in stages, much as they learn to speak and read. In *Spelling Workout,* they move gradually from simple sound/letter relationships to strategies involving more complex word-structure patterns. The use of a sports format motivates and maintains student interest.

Sample Core Lesson

- *Preceding the core lessons are five lessons that feature alphabet and letter review.*

- *A **Get Ready** reading selection uses spelling words in context.*

- ***Get Set** presents the spelling pattern or patterns, providing a lesson focus.*

- *The "Coach" introduces the **Go!** section, which gives students an opportunity to practice new words.*

- *The **List Words** box contains high-frequency spelling words.*

Name _____

Long e Sound

LESSON 23

Get Ready

Read the sentences.

Would you like to see more birds in your yard? If so, feed them! Birds will **eat** lots of foods. Seeds or crumbs make a great bird **meal.** Birds also like apples. Hang an apple from the branch of a **tree.** Try to count how many new birds come to visit!

Get Set

Read the sentences again. Say each word in dark print. Listen for the long **e** sound.

> You can hear the long **e** sound in **tree.** What sound do you hear in the words **eat** and **meal?**

93

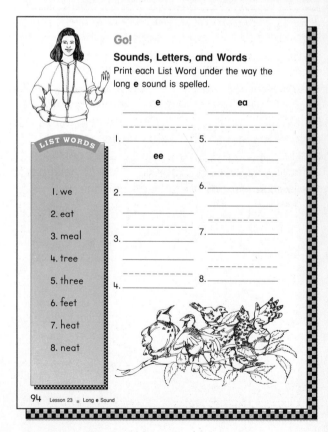

Go!
Sounds, Letters, and Words
Print each List Word under the way the long **e** sound is spelled.

e	ea
1. _____	5. _____
ee	
2. _____	6. _____
3. _____	7. _____
4. _____	8. _____

LIST WORDS

1. we
2. eat
3. meal
4. tree
5. three
6. feet
7. heat
8. neat

ABC Order

Print each set of List Words in ABC order.

meal   feet   heat

_____ _____ _____

1. _____ _____ _____

eat   three   neat

_____ _____ _____

2. _____ _____ _____

Riddles

Print a List Word to answer each riddle.
The word shapes will help you.

1. You and I are this.

2. Breakfast is one.

3. You walk with these.

4. Birds sit in it.

5. You feel it when you sit next to a fire.

6. Two apples and one more

Lesson 23   Long e Sound   95

- A variety of activities provide many opportunities to practice List Words.

- Word puzzles and games help to motivate students.

List Words			
we	meal	three	heat
eat	tree	feet	neat

Proofreading

Read the story. Four List Words are spelled wrong. Circle each one. Then print each word correctly on the line.

Proofreading Marks
⬭ spelling mistake

   My sister and I have a playhouse in a tre. Wie play games there. We like to ete our lunch there. We keep our playhouse clean and neet.

1. _____   3. _____

2. _____   4. _____

Spelling Superstar

Writing

Look at the birds in the tree.
Write a poem about them.
Use List Words in your poem.

96   Lesson 23 ▪ Long e Sound

- *Spelling Superstar* provides opportunities for students to write their spelling words in a variety of writing forms and genres.

Sample Review Lesson

- The **Instant Replay** lesson allows students to review what they've learned.

- **Time Out,** signaled by the "Coach," briefly reviews the spelling patterns used in the previous lessons.

- A variety of activities provide practice and review of selected List Words from the previous lessons.

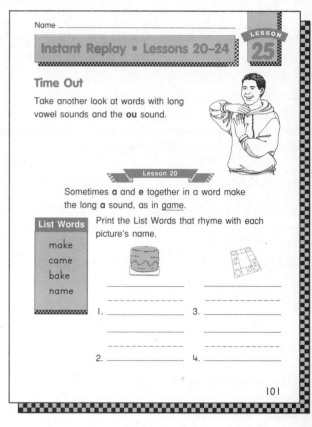

Spelling Workout in the Classroom

Classroom Management

Spelling Workout is designed as a flexible instructional program. The following plans are two ways the program can be taught.

The 5–day Plan
Day 1 – Get Ready/Get Set/Pretest
Day 2 and 3 – Go!
Day 4 – Spelling Superstar
Day 5 – Final Test

The 3–day Plan
Day 1 – Get Ready/Get Set/Pretest/Go!
Day 2 – Go!/Spelling Superstar
Day 3 – Final Test

Testing

Testing is accomplished in several ways. A pretest is administered after reading the Get Ready selection and a final test at the end of each lesson. Dictation sentences for each pretest and final test are provided.

Research suggests that students benefit from correcting their own pretests. After the pretest has been administered, have students self-correct their tests by checking the words against the List Words. You may also want to guide students by reading each letter of the word, asking students to point to each letter and circle any incorrect letters. Then have students rewrite each word correctly.

Tests for Instant Replay lessons are provided in the Teacher's Edition as reproducibles following each lesson. These tests provide not only an evaluation tool for teachers, but also added practice in taking standardized tests for students.

Individualizing Instruction

All-Star Words are provided in the Teacher's Edition for every core lesson as a challenge for better spellers and to provide extension and enrichment for all students.

Review pages called Instant Replay lessons reinforce correct spelling of difficult words from previous lessons.

Students can write misspelled words on Spelling Notebook pages at the back of their books. Students can then use the pages to create a separate notebook of spelling words to use for writing.

A reproducible individual Student Record Chart provided in the Teacher's Edition allows students to record their test scores.

Ideas for meeting the needs of ESL students are provided.

Dictionary

In the back of each student book is a comprehensive dictionary with definitions of all List Words and All-Star Words. Students will have this resource at their fingertips for any assignment.

The Teacher's Edition —Everything You Need!

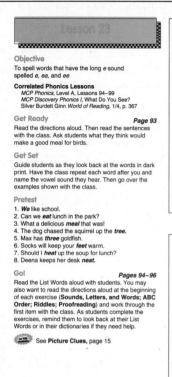

- The goals of each core lesson are clearly stated.

- Spelling lessons are correlated to MCP Phonics, MCP Discovery Phonics I and II, and Silver Burdett Ginn New Dimensions in the World of Reading. Page references refer to Teacher's Edition pages.

- For each reading selection, ideas are provided to prompt students to use the spelling words in an after-reading discussion.

- A **pretest** is administered before the start of each lesson. Dictation sentences are provided.

- Concise teaching notes give guidance for working through the lesson.

- Ideas for meeting the needs of **ESL** students are given.

- **Spelling Strategy** activities provide additional support for reinforcing and analyzing spelling patterns.

- Suggestions for ways students can publish their writing complete the **Writing** activity.

- A **Writer's Corner** extends the content of each reading selection by suggesting ways in which students can explore real-world writing.

- A **Final Test** is administered at the end of the lesson. Dictation sentences are provided.

- **All-Star Words** have the same spelling pattern or patterns as the List Words in the lesson.

Instant Replay Test

Name _____

Side A

Read each set of words. Fill in the circle next to the word that is spelled correctly.

1. ⓐ baik ⓒ bak
   ⓑ backe ⓓ bake

2. ⓐ fiev ⓒ fiv
   ⓑ five ⓓ fivv

3. ⓐ toe ⓒ tooe
   ⓑ tou ⓓ toa

4. ⓐ feete ⓒ feit
   ⓑ feet ⓓ fet

5. ⓐ make ⓒ makk
   ⓑ maik ⓓ macke

6. ⓐ dimme ⓒ dime
   ⓑ diem ⓓ dimm

7. ⓐ oure ⓒ ourr
   ⓑ our ⓓ owr

76

- *Instant Replay lessons review spelling objectives, give guidance for further practice of List Words, and provide dictation sentences for a **Final Replay Test**. Reproducible two-page standardized tests to help prepare students for test-taking are supplied for assessment purposes after each Instant Replay lesson.*

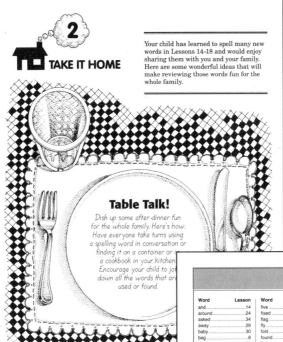

2
TAKE IT HOME

Your child has learned to spell many new words in Lessons 14–18 and would enjoy sharing them with you and your family. Here are some wonderful ideas that will make reviewing those words fun for the whole family.

Table Talk!

Dish up some after-dinner fun for the whole family. Here's how. Have everyone take turns using a spelling word in conversation or finding it on a container or [in] a cookbook in your kitchen. Encourage your child to jot down all the words that are used or found.

62 Take It Home Master ■ Lessons 14–18

List Words

Word	Lesson	Word	Lesson	Word	Lesson	Word	Lesson
and	14	five	21	mine	21	spot	28
around	24	fixed	34	mix	12	star	28
asked	34	flag	27	mother	32	stay	30
away	29	fly	21	mouse	24	stop	7
baby	30	fold	22	my	29	sun	16
bag	8	found	24	name	20	sunny	30
bake	20	from	26	neat	23	take	20
bat	6	fun	8	needed	34	ten	18
bath	32	funny	30	nest	9	they	29
being	35	game	20	not	17	this	15
big	15	gave	20	off	17	three	23
bike	21	glad	27	our	24	time	21
black	27	going	35	out	24	toad	22
blowing	35	got	17	passed	34	toe	22
blue	27	green	26	pay	29	top	12
book	12	grow	26	pen	9	train	26
both	22	hand	14	pig	8	trap	26
box	12	happy	30	pin	7	tree	23
broke	26	has	14	place	20	try	29
brown	26	hat	14	play	27	tub	6
bus	6	having	35	pony	30	us	6
but	16	heat	23	pop	12	van	11
came	20	hit	15	pulled	34	very	11
can	10	home	22	puppy	30	wanted	34
car	10	hook	7	queen	11	we	23
child	33	hop	7	red	18	went	18
chop	33	hot	7	rest	18	wet	10
clay	27	house	24	ride	21	when	32
clock	27	how	24	road	22	where	32
cold	10	hug	16	rope	22	white	32
cooked	34	jar	8	rowing	35	why	32
cry	29	jet	18	rug	10	will	10
day	29	job	17	run	16	win	15
den	15	jog	8	see	6	with	32
did	15	jump	16	she	33	you	11
dime	21	just	16	shoe	33	zip	11
dish	33	kite	21	shop	33	zoo	11
dog	9	lamp	14	show	33		
doing	35	last	28	singing	35		
down	24	leg	9	sit	6		
drink	26	like	21	six	12		
drop	17	looked	34	sky	29		
duck	9	lot	17	sleeping	35		
eat	23	lunch	33	slide	28		
end	18	make	20	slow	28		
fan	8	man	14	small	28		
father	32	many	30	snow	28		
feet	23	map	7	soap	22		
fill	15	meal	23	spoon	28		

150

- *Reproducible **Take It Home Masters** that also follow each Instant Replay lesson strengthen the school-home connection by providing ideas for parents and students for additional practice at home.*

- *Suggested games and group activities make spelling more fun.*

Meeting the Needs of Your ESL Students

Spelling Strategies for Your ESL Students

You may want to try some of these suggestions to help you promote successful language learning for ESL students.

- Prompt use of spelling words by showing pictures or objects that relate to the topic of each selection. Invite students to discuss the picture or object.

- Demonstrate actions or act out words. Encourage students to do the same.

- Read each selection aloud before asking students to read it independently.

- Define words in context and allow students to offer their own meanings of words.

- Make the meanings of words concrete by naming objects or pictures, role-playing, or pantomiming.

Spelling is the relationship between sounds and letters. Learning to spell words in English is an interesting challenge for English First Language speakers as well as English as a Second Language speakers. You may want to adapt some of the following activities to accommodate the needs of your students—both native and non-English speakers.

Rhymes and Songs

Use rhymes, songs, poems, or chants to introduce new letter sounds and spelling words. Repeat the rhyme or song several times during the day or week, having students listen to you first, then repeat back to you line by line. To enhance learning for visual learners in your classroom and provide opportunities for pointing out letter combinations and their sounds, you may want to write the rhyme, song, poem, or chant on the board. As you examine the words, students can easily see similarities and differences among them. Encourage volunteers to select and recite a rhyme or sing a song for the class. Students may enjoy some of the selections in *Miss Mary Mack and Other Children's Street Rhymes* by Joanna Cole and Stephanie Calmenson or *And the Green Grass Grew All Around* by Alvin Schwartz.

Student Dictation

To take advantage of individual students' known vocabulary, suggest that students build their own sentences incorporating the List Words. For example:

Mary ran.
Mary ran away.
Mary ran away quickly.

Sentence building can expand students' knowledge of how to spell words and of how to notice language patterns, learn descriptive words, and so on.

Words in Context

Using words in context sentences will aid students' mastery of new vocabulary.

- Say several sentences using the List Words in context and have students repeat after you. Encourage more proficient students to make up sentences using List Words that you suggest.

- Write cloze sentences on the board and have students help you complete them with the List Words.

Point out the spelling patterns in the words, using colored chalk to underline or circle the elements.

Oral Drills

Use oral drills to help students make associations among sounds and the letters that represent them. You might use oral drills at listening stations to reinforce the language, allowing ESL students to listen to the drills at their own pace.

Spelling Aloud   Say each List Word and have students repeat the word. Next, write it on the board as you name each letter, then say the word again as you track the letters and sound by sweeping your hand under the word. Call attention to spelling changes for words to which endings or suffixes were added. For words with more than one syllable, emphasize each syllable as you write, encouraging students to clap out the syllables. Ask volunteers to repeat the procedure.

Variant Spellings   For a group of words that contain the same vowel sound, but variant spellings, write an example on the board, say the word, and then present other words in that word family *(cake: rake, bake, lake).* Point out the sound and the letter(s) that stand for the sound. Then add words to the list that have the same vowel sound *(play, say, day).* Say pairs of words *(cake, play)* as you point to them, and identify the vowel sound and the different letters that represent the sound *(long a: a_e, ay).* Ask volunteers to select a different pair of words and repeat the procedure.

Vary this activity by drawing a chart on the board that shows the variant spellings for a sound. Invite students to add words under the correct spelling pattern. Provide a list of words for students to choose from to help those ESL students with limited vocabularies.

Categorizing To help students discriminate among consonant sounds and spellings, have them help you categorize words with single consonant sounds and consonant blends or digraphs. For example, ask students to close their eyes so that they may focus solely on the sounds in the words, and then pronounce *smart, smile, spend,* and *special.* Next, pronounce the words as you write them on the board. After spelling each word, create two columns—one for *sm,* one for *sp.* Have volunteers pronounce each word, decide which column it fits under, and write the word in the correct column. Encourage students to add to the columns any other words they know that have those consonant blends.

To focus on initial, medial, or final consonant sounds, point out the position of the consonant blends or digraphs in the List Words. Have students find and list the words under columns labeled *Beginning, Middle, End.*

Tape Recording Encourage students to work with a partner or their group to practice their spelling words. If a tape recorder is available, students can practice at their own pace by taking turns recording the words, playing back the tape, and writing each word they hear. Students can then help each other check their spelling against their *Spelling Workout* books. Observe as needed to be sure students are spelling the words correctly.

Comparing/Contrasting To help students focus on word parts, write List Words with prefixes or suffixes on the board and have volunteers circle, underline, or draw a line between the prefix or suffix and its root word. Review the meaning of each root word, then invite students to work with their group to write two sentences: one using just the root word; the other using the root word with its prefix or suffix. For example: *My favorite mystery was* due *at the library Monday afternoon. By Tuesday afternoon the book was* overdue! Or, *You can* depend *on Jen to arrive for softball practice on time. She is* dependable. Have students contrast the two sentences, encouraging them to tell how the prefix or suffix changed the meaning of the root word.

Questions/Answers Write List Words on the board and ask pairs of students to brainstorm questions or answers about the words, such as "Which word names more than one? How do you know?" (foxes, *an* es *was added at the end)* or, "Which word tells that something belongs to the children? How do you know?" (children's *is spelled with an* 's)

Games

You may want to invite students to participate in these activities.

Picture Clues Students can work with a partner to draw pictures or cut pictures out of magazines that represent the List Words, then trade papers and label each other's pictures. Encourage students to check each other's spelling against their *Spelling Workout* books.

Or, you can present magazine cutouts or items that picture the List Words. As you display each picture or item, say the word clearly and then write it on the board as you spell it aloud. Non-English speakers may wish to know the translation of the word in their native language so that they can mentally connect the new word with a familiar one. Students may also find similarities in the spellings of the words.

Letter Cards Have students create letter cards for vowels, vowel digraphs, consonants, consonant blends and digraphs, and so on. Then say a List Word and have students show the card that has the letters representing the sound for the vowels or consonants in that word as they repeat and spell the word after you. Students can use their cards independently as they work with their group.

Charades/Pantomime Students can use gestures and actions to act out the List Words. To receive credit for a correctly guessed word, players must spell the word correctly. Such activities can be played in pairs so that beginning English speakers will not feel pressured. If necessary, translate the words into students' native languages so that they understand the meanings of the words before attempting to act them out.

Change or No Change Have students make flash cards for root words and endings. One student holds up a root word; another holds up an ending. The class says "Change" or "No Change" to describe what happens when the root word and ending are combined. Encourage students to spell the word with its ending added.

Scope and Sequence for MCP Spelling Workout

Skills	Level A	Level B	Level C	Level D	Level E	Level F	Level G	Level H
Consonants	1–12	1–2	1–2	1	1	1, 7, 9	RC	RC
Short Vowels	14–18	3–5	4	2	RC	RC	RC	RC
Long Vowels	20–23	7–11	5, 7	3	RC	RC	RC	RC
Consonant Blends/Clusters	26–28	13–14	8–9 29	5, 7	RC	RC	RC	RC
y as a Vowel	29–30	15–16	10–11	RC	RC	RC	RC	RC
Consonant Digraphs—**th, ch, sh, wh, ck**	32–33	28–29 32	27–28 31	9	RC	RC	RC	RC
Vowel Digraphs		25–26 33	21–22 25	19–22	7–10	11 13–16 19	25	RC
R–Controlled Vowels		19–20	13–14	8	RC	RC	RC	RC
Diphthongs	24	27	26	22–23	11	16–17	RC	RC
Silent Consonants			23	10	4	4–5	RC	RC
Hard and Soft **c** and **g**		32	3	4	2	2	RC	RC
Plurals			19–20	25–27 29	33–34	33	RC	RC
Prefixes		34	32–33	31–32	13–17	20–23 25	7–8	7–11 19–20
Suffixes	34–35	21–23	15–17	13–17	25–29 31–32	26–29 31–32	9 13–14 16, 26	5, 25–27
Contractions		17	34	28	23	RC	RC	RC
Possessives				28–29	23	RC	RC	RC
Compound Words				33	19	RC	RC	RC
Synonyms/Antonyms				34	RC	RC	RC	RC
Homonyms		35	35	35	RC	RC	RC	RC
Spellings of /f/ **f, ff, ph, gh**				11	3	3	RC	RC
Syllables					20–23	RC	RC	RC
Commonly Misspelled Words					35	34	17, 35	17, 29 35
Abbreviations						35	RC	RC
Latin Roots							11, 15 31	13–16

Skills	Level A	Level B	Level C	Level D	Level E	Level F	Level G	Level H
Words with French or Spanish Derivations							10, 29	RC
Words of Latin/French/Greek Origin								21–23 28
Latin Prefixes							33	RC
List Words Related to Specific Curriculum Areas							19–23 28, 32	31–34
Vocabulary Development	●	●	●	●	●	●	●	●
Dictionary	●	●	●	●	●	●	●	●
Writing	●	●	●	●	●	●	●	●
Proofreading	●	●	●	●	●	●	●	●
Literature Selections	●	●	●	●	●	●	●	●
All-Star Words	●	●	●	●	●	●	●	●
Review Tests in Standardized Format	●	●	●	●	●	●	●	●

Spelling Through Writing

Skills	Level A	Level B	Level C	Level D	Level E	Level F	Level G	Level H
Poetry	●	●	●	●	●	●	●	●
Narrative Writings	●	●	●	●	●	●	●	●
Descriptive Writings	●	●	●	●	●	●	●	●
Expository Writings	●	●	●	●	●	●	●	●
Persuasive Writings			●	●	●	●		
Notes/Letters	●	●	●		●	●	●	●
Riddles/Jokes	●		●					
Recipes	●	●	●			●	●	
Newspaper Articles		●	●	●	●	●		●
Conversations/Dialogues				●	●	●		●
Menus						●	●	
Questionnaires		●			●	●	●	●
Logs/Journals			●	●	●	●	●	
Advertisements		●	●	●	●	●	●	●
Reports					●	●	●	●
Literary Devices							●	●
Scripts							●	●
Speeches						●		●

Numbers in chart indicate lesson numbers
RC = reinforced in other contexts
● = found throughout

Lesson 1

Objective
To identify which pictures have names that begin or end with the same sound

Presenting the Lesson
Page 5

You may want to name each new coach for students. Knowing their names will add interest to the lessons.

Say the words *top* and *ten* and ask who can tell something about the beginnings of the two words. After a volunteer states that both words begin with the sound of *t*, continue the procedure with other pairs of familiar words such as *run, red; cat, cup; fox, fish;* etc.

Next have the class listen while you say the words *sun, ten, top,* and *sit*. Have a volunteer give one pair of the words that has the same beginning sound and then ask another student to give another pair of words with the same beginning sound. Repeat the procedure with other familiar words such as *fine, fun, goat, gum; pit, jump, jam, pan; yell, zero, zipper, yawn;* etc. Introduce the activity by reading the directions aloud and working through the first item with the class. Then have students complete the page.

Page 6

Say the words *far* and *deer* and ask a volunteer to tell something about the endings of the words. After a student states that the two words both end with the same sound of *r*, continue the procedure with other pairs of familiar words such as *bag, hog; jeep, rap; jam, rim;* etc. Introduce the activity by reading the directions aloud and working through the first item with the class. Then have students complete the page.

Beginning and Ending Sounds

Say the names of the pictures in each box. Which ones have the same **beginning** sound? Draw a line to connect the pictures with the same **beginning** sound.

5

Say the names of the pictures in each box. Which ones have the same **ending** sound? Draw a line to connect the pictures with the same **ending** sound.

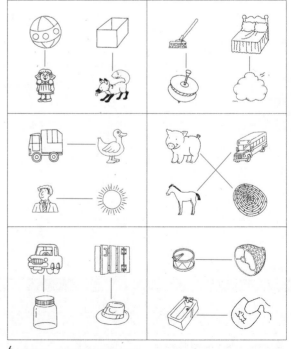

6   Lesson I   Beginning and Ending Sounds

Say the name of the first picture in the row. Circle each picture in the row with the same **beginning** sound as the first picture.

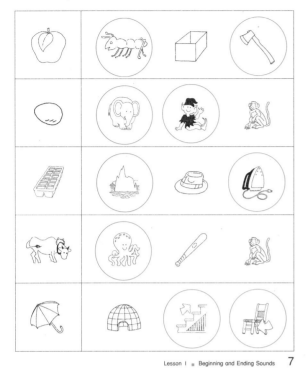

Ask the class to listen closely to the words *and, boy, at*. Have a student name two of the words that begin with the same sound as the word *apple*. Continue this procedure for each of the other vowel sounds on the page: short *e* (*egg—echo, every, gate*); short *o* (*ox—piano, odd, on*); short *u* (*umbrella—umpire, upset, state*); and long *i* (*ice—island, horse, icicle*). Introduce the activity by reading the directions aloud and working through the first item with the class. Then have students complete the page.

Page 8

Ask the class to listen to the words *choose, china, collar*. Then ask which two words begin with the same sound. After a student identifies the words *choose* and *china*, continue the procedure with other groups of familiar words such as *trap, rain, trail; shock, sharp, stove;* etc. Introduce the activity by reading the directions aloud and working through the first item with the class. Then have students complete the page.

Say the name of the first picture in the row. Circle each picture in the row with the same **beginning** sound as the first picture.

Lesson 2

Objective
To match each capital letter with its partner small letter form and vice versa, arrange the letters in alphabetical order, and write the capital letter forms

Correlated Phonics Lessons
Silver Burdett Ginn *World of Reading,* 1/1, pp. 21–50

Presenting the Lesson

Page 9

Write a capital or small letter on the board and have students find both forms of the same letter on their page. Then have them name a word that begins with the letters and give other words with the same beginning sound (*except for* X). If additional reinforcement is indicated, have each student trace the identified letters in both forms. Follow this procedure for each letter of the alphabet.

Page 10

Call on a volunteer to name the letters in the first box—first the single letter on the left and then the letters to the right. Have the rest of the class put their fingers on each letter as it is named. After working through the second box, read the directions for page 10 with students and have them complete the activity. If additional reinforcement is indicated, work through all the boxes on the page with the class.

Alphabet Review

LESSON 2

Look at the partner letters, capital and small. Say the letters.

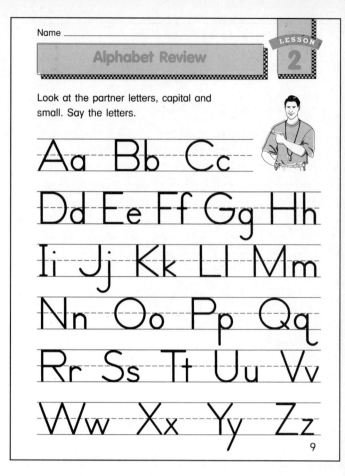

Aa Bb Cc
Dd Ee Ff Gg Hh
Ii Jj Kk Ll Mm
Nn Oo Pp Qq
Rr Ss Tt Uu Vv
Ww Xx Yy Zz

9

Look at the letter in the circle. Then circle the letter that is just like it at the right.

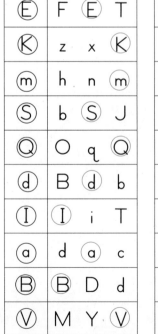
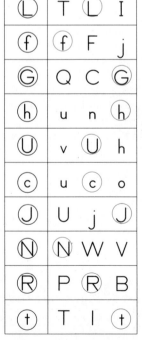

Ⓔ	F	Ⓔ	T
Ⓚ	z	x	Ⓚ
ⓜ	h	n	ⓜ
Ⓢ	b	Ⓢ	J
Ⓠ	O	q	Ⓠ
ⓓ	B	ⓓ	b
Ⓘ	Ⓘ	i	T
ⓐ	d	ⓐ	c
Ⓑ	Ⓑ	D	d
Ⓥ	M	Y	Ⓥ

Ⓛ	T	Ⓛ	I
ⓕ	ⓕ	F	j
Ⓖ	Q	C	Ⓖ
ⓗ	u	n	ⓗ
Ⓤ	v	Ⓤ	h
ⓒ	u	ⓒ	o
Ⓙ	U	j	Ⓙ
Ⓝ	Ⓝ	W	V
Ⓡ	P	Ⓡ	B
ⓣ	T	I	ⓣ

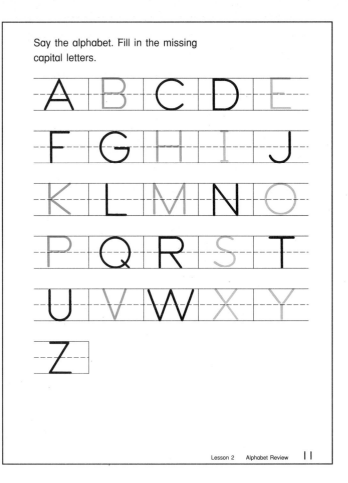

Say the alphabet. Fill in the missing capital letters.

A B C D E
F G H I J
K L M N O
P Q R S T
U V W X Y
Z

First refer students to page 9. Call on volunteers to name the capital letters of the alphabet in their order of occurrence. Ask students which letter comes before *J;* which letter comes after *C;* which letter comes between *M* and *O;* and so forth, to give students practice in specific alphabetical location. When the class is familiar with the alphabet, read the directions for page 11 with students and have them complete the activity.

Call on a volunteer to name the letters in the first box in the left-hand column—first the single letter on the left and then the letters to the right. Have the rest of the class put their fingers on each letter as it is named. Work through the second box with students. Then read the directions for the left-hand column and have students complete the activity. If additional reinforcement is indicated, work through all the boxes in the column with the class. Repeat the procedure for the boxes in the right-hand column.

Look at the capital letter. Circle its small partner letter.

X	y	z	(x)
A	(a)	V	H
Q	(q)	g	o
D	b	(d)	p
F	j	E	(f)
H	(h)	n	b
M	w	n	(m)
R	(r)	P	k
P	(p)	b	d
T	l	(t)	I

Look at the small letter. Circle its capital partner letter.

w	(W)	M	v
y	V	(Y)	g
z	N	(Z)	W
b	D	P	(B)
e	C	c	(E)
g	q	(G)	Q
i	j	(I)	L
j	(J)	i	U
k	C	R	(K)
n	M	(N)	h

Lesson 3

Objective

To associate the letters *A* through *N* with the initial sound in picture names and to write the letters in capital and small forms

Correlated Phonics Lessons

Silver Burdett Ginn *World of Reading,* 1/1, pp. 21–50

Presenting the Lesson   *Page 13*

Call on a volunteer to name the first picture on the left. Then have the class repeat the name of the picture and listen for the beginning sound. Next write the name of the picture on the board and have a student name the letter associated with the beginning sound. Direct students to find both forms of the letter in their books. Then, as you write both forms of the letter on the board, have students trace each letter in their books with their fingers. After they have completed each line on page 13 orally, have students name each letter aloud, trace the letter with their fingers, trace the letter with their pencils, and finally write the letter at least three more times on the lines in their books.

Page 14

Use as much of the direction from page 13 as you think necessary for students to complete page 14.

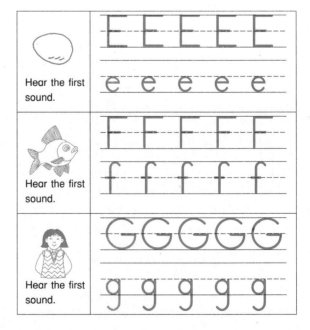

Say the name of the picture.
Trace the letter of the first sound.
Then print the letter.

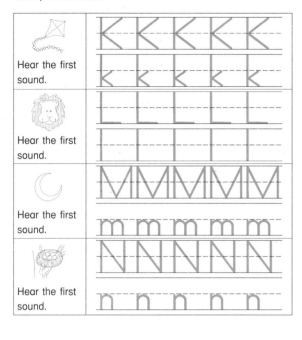

Hear the first sound.	K K K K
	k k k k
Hear the first sound.	L L L L
	L L L L
Hear the first sound.	M M M M
	m m m m
Hear the first sound.	N N N N
	n n n n

Use as much of the direction from page 13 as you think necessary for students to complete page 15.

Use as much of the direction from page 13 as you think necessary for students to complete page 16.

Say the name of the picture.
Trace the letter of the first sound.
Then print the letter.

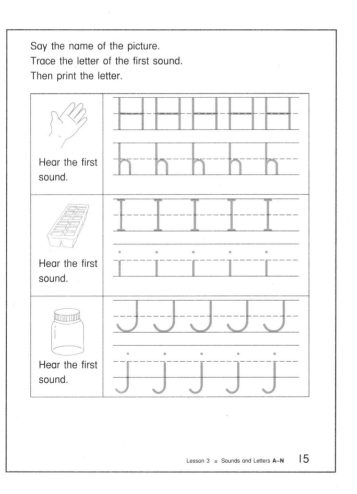

Hear the first sound.	H H H H H
	h h h h h
Hear the first sound.	I I I I I
	i i i i i
Hear the first sound.	J J J J J
	j j j j j

Lesson 4

Objective

To associate the letters *O* through *Z* with the initial or final sound in picture names and to write the letters in capital and small forms

Correlated Phonics Lessons

Silver Burdett Ginn *World of Reading,* 1/1, pp. 21–50

Presenting the Lesson

Page 17

Call on a volunteer to name the first picture on the left. Have the class repeat the name of the picture and listen for the beginning sound. Next write the name of the picture on the board and have a student name the letter associated with the beginning sound. Direct students to find both forms of the letter in their books. Then, as you write both forms of the letter on the board, have students trace each line in their books with their fingers. After they have completed each line on page 17 orally, have students name each letter aloud, trace the letter with their fingers, trace the letter with their pencils, and finally write the letter at least three more times on the lines in their books.

Page 18

Use as much of the direction from page 17 as you think necessary for students to complete page 18.

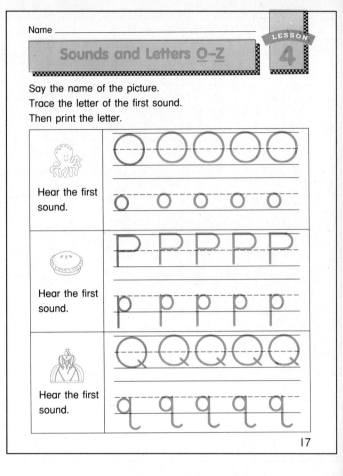

Sounds and Letters O–Z

LESSON 4

Say the name of the picture.
Trace the letter of the first sound.
Then print the letter.

Hear the first sound.

Hear the first sound.

Hear the first sound.

17

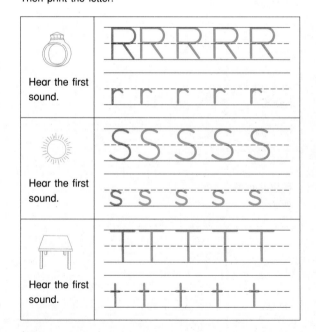

Say the name of the picture.
Trace the letter of the first sound.
Then print the letter.

Hear the first sound.

Hear the first sound.

Hear the first sound.

18   Lesson 4 ▪ Sounds and Letters O–Z

Say the name of the picture.
Trace the letter of the first sound.
Then print the letter.

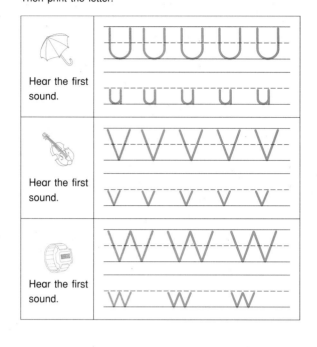

Hear the first sound.	U U U U U u u u u u
Hear the first sound.	V V V V V v v v v v
Hear the first sound.	W W W W W W

Use as much of the direction from page 17 as you think necessary for students to complete page 19. Explain to students that because of the size of the letter *W*, they will not be able to write as many *W*'s as the other letters.

Use as much of the direction from page 17 as you think necessary for students to complete page 20.

Say the name of the picture.
Trace the letter of the sound.
Then print the letter.

Hear the **last** sound.	X X X X X x x x x x
Hear the first sound.	Y Y Y Y Y y y y y y
Hear the first sound.	Z Z Z Z Z z z z z z

Lesson 5

Objective
To identify the initial and final letters of selected picture names

Correlated Phonics Lessons
MCP Phonics, Level A, Lessons 1–4
Silver Burdett Ginn *World of Reading,* 1/1, pp. 38–39

Presenting the Lesson   *Page 21*
Name three words that begin with the same consonant sound, such as *boy, bell,* and *bat*. Have the class repeat the three words and listen for the beginning sound. Then have a volunteer tell what is the same about the words (*they all begin with the sound of* b) and have another student name the letter associated with that sound (*b*). Repeat this procedure using different initial sounds. Then call on a student to name the letters on the left in the first item and say the names of the pictures across the row. Ask the class which letter stands for the beginning sound of all three picture names (*f*). Finally, read the directions for page 21 with students and have them complete the page.

Page 22

Name three words that end with the same sound, such as *pig, bag,* and *hug*. Have the class repeat the three words and listen for the ending sound. Have a volunteer tell what is the same about the words (*they all end with the sound of* g) and have another student name the letter associated with that sound (*g*). Repeat this procedure using different final sounds. Then call on a student to name the letters on the right in the first item and say the names of the pictures across the row. Ask the class which letter stands for the ending sound of all three words (*r*). Finally, read the directions for page 22 with students and have them complete the page.

Matching Sounds and Letters

Say the name of each picture.
How does each start? Circle the letter that stands for the beginning sound.

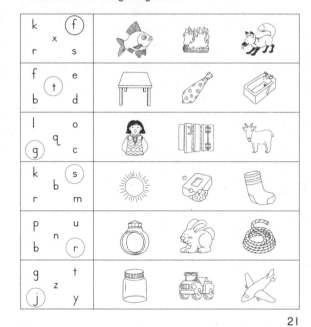

21

Say the name of each picture.
How does each end? Circle the letter that stands for the ending sound.

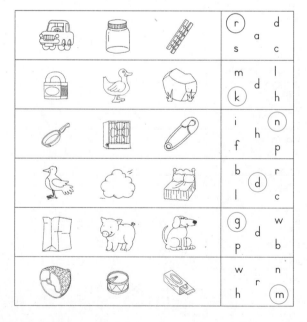

Say the name of each picture in the box. How does it start? Draw a line to connect the picture with the letter that stands for its beginning sound.

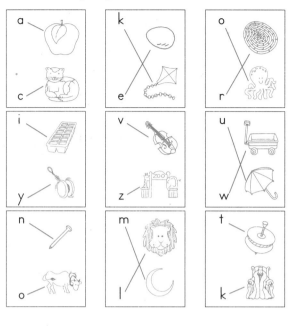

Name a word beginning with a single consonant sound, such as *dog.* Have the class repeat the word and listen for the beginning sound. Then call on a student to name the letter associated with the sound (*d*) and to name two more words that have the same beginning sound. Next read the directions for page 23 with students and work through the first box at the top left corner of the page with the class. Then have them complete the page on their own.

Page 24

Write the word *hat* on the board and have a volunteer give the beginning and ending sounds and the letters associated with them. Repeat the procedure for *tub, mad, bag,* etc. Next read the directions for page 24 with students and work through the first item with them. Then have them complete the page on their own.

Say the name of each picture. How does it start? Circle the letter. Print the letter of the beginning sound on the line.

Say the name of each picture. How does it end? Circle the letter. Print the letter of the ending sound on the line.

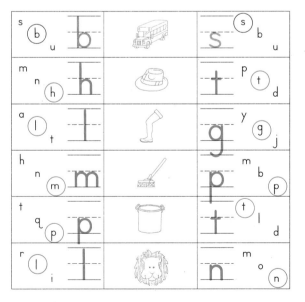

Lesson 6

Objective
To spell words with initial or final *s, t,* or *b*

Correlated Phonics Lessons
MCP Phonics, Level A, Lessons 6–8
MCP Discovery Phonics I, What Do You See?/City
   Rhythms/Little Bunny's Lunch
Silver Burdett Ginn *World of Reading,* 1/1, pp. 27, 88;
   1/2, pp. T91–98

Get Ready   Page 25
Read the directions aloud. Then read the sentences
with the class. Invite students to tell what is
happening in the picture.

Get Set
Guide students as they look back at the words in dark
print. Ask the class to say each word with you and to
name the beginning and ending sounds. Then go over
the examples shown with the class.

Pretest
1. Fill the **tub** with hot, soapy water.
2. Is the school **bus** late?
3. Karen hit a home run with the **bat**.
4. I like to **see** you smile.
5. Let's **sit** down and rest.
6. Thank you for helping **us** paint the fence.

Go!   Pages 26–28
Read the List Words aloud with students. You may
also want to read the directions aloud at the beginning
of each exercise (**Sounds, Letters, and Words;
Beginning Sounds; Ending Sounds; Missing
Words**) and work through the first item with the class.
As students complete the exercises, remind them to
look back at their List Words.

   For the **Sounds, Letters, and Words** exercise, ask
students whether they can name the List Word that
has two meanings—a "wooden club for playing
baseball" and a "small, flying animal" (*bat*).

 See **Categorizing,** page 15

Get Ready
Read the sentences.

   Hello! Hello!
   We **see** the **bus.**
   Hello! Hello!
   Can the bus see us?
   Wave. Make a fuss!
   Here.
   Come **sit** with us!

Get Set
Read the sentences again. Say each word in dark
print. Listen for the beginning and the ending sounds.

 The word **sit** begins with the sound for **s.**
It ends with the sound for **t.**

 The word **bus** begins with the sound for **b.**
It ends with the sound for **s.**

 The word **tub** begins with the sound for **t.**
What sound do you hear at the end of **tub?**

25

Go!
Sounds, Letters, and Words
Look at the pictures. Print the letter that
stands for the missing beginning sound
or ending sound. Trace the letters to
spell List Words.

LIST WORDS

1. tub
2. bus
3. bat
4. see
5. sit
6. us

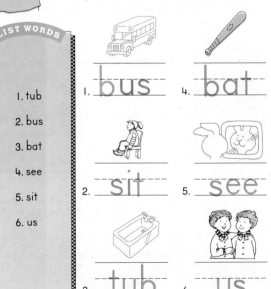

1. bus   4. bat

2. sit   5. see

3. tub   6. us

26   Lesson 6 ▪ Beginning and Ending **s, t, b**

28

Beginning Sounds

Trace each letter. Print a List Word that begins with the sound for the letter.

1. see

2. sit

3. tub

4. bus

5. bat

Ending Sounds

Trace each letter. Print a List Word that ends with the sound for the letter.

6. bus

7. us

8. tub

9. sit

List Words		
tub	bus	bat
see	sit	us

Missing Words

Print the List Word that completes each sentence.

1. Here are a ball and a **bat** .

2. I can **see** how I look.

3. Do they see **us** ?

Spelling Superstar

Writing

What is a good rule for riding on the bus? Make a sign that tells the rule.

◎ **Spelling Strategy**   To help students recognize beginning and ending *s, t,* or *b,* you may want to write *sat, bib,* and *too* on the board. Point out the letters that stand for the beginning sounds of *b, s,* and *t* and the ending sounds of *t* and *b.* Then say each word and invite students to name List Words that have the same beginning and/or ending sounds.

Spelling Superstar   *Page 28*

Offer assistance as needed as students complete the **Writing** activity. Students may want to share their rules by reading them aloud to the class, then posting their signs.

✎ Writer's Corner

You may wish to invite a bus driver to visit the class. Before the visit, ask groups of students to write questions to ask the driver. Afterward, have the class write a thank-you letter.

Final Test

1. Please bring your ball and **bat** to the playground.
2. Will the **bus** stop at the corner?
3. I want to **see** your new puppy.
4. I will **sit** down to read my book.
5. Let's give the dog a bath in that big **tub.**
6. What a delicious meal Dad made for **us!**

Have students check their Final Tests against the List Words. Encourage them to write any misspelled words on their Spelling Notebook pages in the back of their books. Students can use the pages to create a separate notebook of spelling words to use for writing.

★★ All-Star Words

set   tag   boat   cub

After you write the All-Star Words on the board, pronounce them for the class and discuss their meanings. Then say each word below. Invite students to work with a partner to write the All-Star Word that rhymes with the word.

1. met   (set)
2. wag   (tag)
3. coat   (boat)
4. rub   (cub)

Lesson 7

Objective
To spell words with initial or final *h, m, p,* or *k*

Correlated Phonics Lessons
MCP Phonics, Level A, Lessons 10–12, 30
MCP Discovery Phonics I, Who Said Boo?/When the
    Alligator Came to Class/City Rhythms/Little
    Bunny's Lunch
Silver Burdett Ginn *World of Reading,* 1/1, pp. 50, 77;
    1/2, pp. 68, 99

Get Ready   *Page 29*
Read the directions aloud. Then read the sentences
with the class. Invite students to tell you what the
picture shows.

Get Set
Guide students as they look back at the words in dark
print. Ask volunteers to say each word and to name
the beginning and ending sounds. Then go over the
examples shown with the class.

Pretest
1. Is the iron **hot** now?
2. Main Street is shown on this **map.**
3. I will **pin** your name tag to your coat.
4. Pam will catch a fish with that **hook.**
5. The rabbit will **hop** all the way home.
6. I wish the rain would **stop.**

Go!   *Pages 30–32*
Read the List Words aloud with students. You may
also want to read the directions aloud at the beginning
of each exercise (**Sounds, Letters, and Words;
Beginning Sounds; Ending Sounds; Vocabulary**)
and work through the first item with the class. As
students complete the exercises, remind them to look
back at their List Words.

    For the **Beginning Sounds** and **Ending Sounds**
exercises, suggest that students think of objects
whose names begin or end with *h, m, k,* or *p* (*kite,
pan, arm*). Students can draw pictures of the objects
in the white spaces on page 31.

 See **Charades/Pantomime,** page 15

Name _____

Beginning and Ending <u>h</u>, <u>m</u>, <u>p</u>, <u>k</u>

Get Ready
Read the sentences.

The **map** is on a **hook**.
Sara will show us where she lives.
She will **pin** her name on the map.

Get Set
Read the sentences again. Say each
word in dark print. Listen for the
beginning and the ending sounds.

 The word **map** begins with the sound for **m.**
It ends with the sound for **p.**

The word **hook** begins with the sound for **h.**
It ends with the sound for **k.**

What letter stands for the sound at the
beginning of the word **pin**?

Go!
Sounds, Letters, and Words
Look at the pictures. Print the letter that
stands for the missing beginning sound
or ending sound. Trace the letters to
spell List Words.

LIST WORDS

1. hot
2. map
3. pin
4. hook
5. hop
6. stop

1. pin
2. stop
3. hot
4. hop
5. hook
6. map

Beginning Sounds

Name each picture. Print each List Word that begins with the same sound as the picture name.

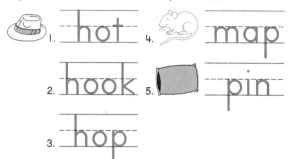

1. hot   4. map

2. hook   5. pin

3. hop

Ending Sounds

Name each picture. Print each List Word that ends with the same sound as the picture name.

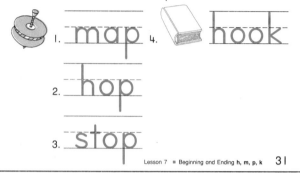

1. map   4. hook

2. hop

3. stop

List Words		
hot	pin	hop
map	hook	stop

Vocabulary

Print the List Word that goes with each clue.

1. It holds something together.   pin

2. How does the sun feel?   hot

3. Do this before crossing a street.   stop

Spelling Superstar

Writing

How can you help a friend find where you live? Write a sentence to tell what you would do.

◎ **Spelling Strategy**   Students may enjoy clearing a space in the classroom, or going to the playground, and bodily spelling out each List Word. Guide the activity by calling out the List Words and helping groups of students arrange themselves into the shapes of the letters in each word.

Spelling Superstar   *Page 32*

Offer assistance as needed as students complete the **Writing** activity. Students may want to share their writing by exchanging sentences with a partner.

✎ Writer's Corner

You may wish to bring a map of your area to the classroom and point out the street on which your school is located. Invite students to write a sentence about their school and the street it is on.

Final Test

1. What fun it is to **hop** on one foot!
2. May I have a cup of **hot** soup?
3. I will **pin** the pair of mittens together.
4. Hang your jacket on a **hook** in your closet.
5. Trains **stop** here every half hour.
6. We drew a **map** of our town.

Remind students to check their Final Tests against the List Words and to write any misspelled words in their Spelling Notebook.

★★ All-Star Words

pup   him   cook   milk

Write the All-Star Words on the board as you pronounce each word and discuss its meaning. Then invite students to work with a partner to say each word, name its beginning and ending sound or sounds, and then write the word.

Lesson 8

Objective
To spell words with initial or final *j, f,* or *g*

Correlated Phonics Lessons
MCP Phonics, Level A, Lessons 16–18
MCP Discovery Phonics I, The Baby Who Got All the
 Blame/Best Friends
Silver Burdett Ginn *World of Reading,* 1/2, pp. 50, 69

Get Ready   *Page 33*
Read the directions aloud. Then read the poem with
the class. Ask students whether or not they would
enjoy having a pig for a pet.

Get Set
Guide students as they look back at the words in dark
print. Ask the class to say each word with you and to
name the beginning and ending sounds. Then go over
the examples shown with the class.

Pretest
1. Did you remember to buy a *jar* of peanut butter?
2. It was so hot I turned on the *fan.*
3. What *fun* it is to jump rope!
4. I carried a big *bag* of groceries.
5. Mom likes to *jog* in the morning.
6. The little *pig* made a loud squeal.

Go!   *Pages 34–36*
Read the List Words aloud with students. You may
also want to read the directions aloud at the beginning
of each exercise (**Sounds, Letters, and Words;
Matching; Vocabulary; Sentence Completion**) and
work through the first item with the class. As students
complete the exercises, remind them to look back at
their List Words.

  For the **Sounds, Letters, and Words** exercise,
emphasize that beginning letters are written at the left
of a word and ending letters are written at the right.

 See **Picture Clues,** page 15

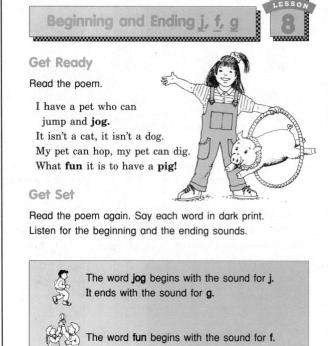

Beginning and Ending *j, f, g*   LESSON 8

Get Ready
Read the poem.

  I have a pet who can
   jump and **jog.**
  It isn't a cat, it isn't a dog.
  My pet can hop, my pet can dig.
  What **fun** it is to have a **pig!**

Get Set
Read the poem again. Say each word in dark print.
Listen for the beginning and the ending sounds.

> The word **jog** begins with the sound for **j.**
> It ends with the sound for **g.**
>
> The word **fun** begins with the sound for **f.**
>
> What letter stands for the sound at the end
> of the word **pig?**

33

Go!
Sounds, Letters, and Words
Look at the pictures. Print the letter that
stands for the missing beginning sound
or ending sound. Trace the letters to
spell List Words.

LIST WORDS

1. jar
2. fan
3. fun
4. bag
5. jog
6. pig

1. bag   4. fun
2. fan   5. jar
3. pig   6. jog

Matching

Look at each picture. Then print a List Word to name each picture.

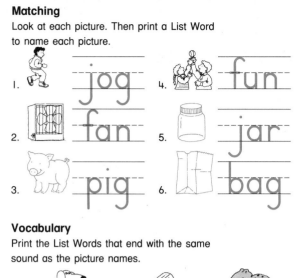

1. jog
2. fan
3. pig
4. fun
5. jar
6. bag

Vocabulary

Print the List Words that end with the same sound as the picture names.

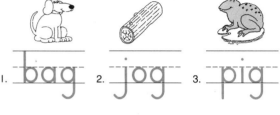

1. bag
2. jog
3. pig

List Words		
jar	fun	jog
fan	bag	pig

Sentence Completion

Look at each picture. Print the List Word that completes each sentence.

1. The **jar** is in the bag.

2. It is **fun** to play.

3. Turn on the **fan**.

Spelling Superstar

Writing

It is fun to see the pets people have. Write a sentence about one of the pets in the pictures.

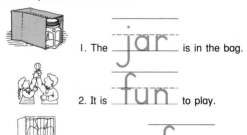

 **Spelling Strategy** To give students practice with the letters *j, f,* and *g,* say *jar* and *jog* and ask students what is the same about the two words. After you write the words on the board, repeat the question. Then call on a volunteer to underline the *j* in each word. Continue this procedure for words with initial *f* (*fan, fun*) and final *g* (*bag, jog, pig*).

Spelling Superstar   *Page 36*

Offer assistance as needed as students complete the **Writing** activity. Students may want to share their work by reading their sentences aloud to a partner.

✍ Writer's Corner

> Students may enjoy listening to the story *Perfect the Pig* by Susan Jeschke. After you finish, ask students to write a sentence about the part of the story they liked the best.

Final Test

1. Guess how many beans are in the *jar.*
2. A *pig* can make a good pet.
3. I *jog* two miles every day.
4. Did you have *fun* at the zoo?
5. My lunch is in that paper *bag.*
6. The *fan* blew papers around the room.

Remind students to check their Final Tests against the List Words and to write any misspelled words in their Spelling Notebook.

★★ All-Star Words

joke   food   fat   girl

After you write the All-Star Words on the board, pronounce them for the class and discuss their meanings. Then say each word below. With a partner, students can write the All-Star Word that has the same beginning sound as the word.

1. gate   (girl)
2. jeep   (joke)
3. fold   (food or fat)

Lesson 9

Objective

To spell words with initial or final *l, d,* or *n*

Correlated Phonics Lessons

MCP Phonics, Level A, Lessons 20–22
MCP Discovery Phonics I, What Do You See?/Who Said Boo?/The Popcorn Popper
Silver Burdett Ginn *World of Reading,* 1/1, p. 28; 1/2, pp. 51, 91

Get Ready   *Page 37*

Read the directions aloud. Then read the sentences with the class. Ask students to name the animal homes that the sentences and pictures tell about.

Get Set

Guide students as they look back at the words in dark print. Ask volunteers to say each word and to name the beginning and ending sounds. Then go over the examples shown with the class.

Pretest

1. Diane fell and hurt her *leg.*
2. Is Ned's pet a big, white *dog?*
3. My *pen* is out of ink.
4. A *duck* can swim and fly.
5. Birds live in a *nest.*
6. Never go into a lion's *den!*

Go!   *Pages 38–40*

Read the List Words aloud with students. You may also want to read the directions aloud at the beginning of each exercise (**Sounds, Letters, and Words; Missing Letters; Vocabulary; Rhyming; Picture Puzzle**) and work through the first item with the class. As students complete the exercises, remind them to look back at their List Words.

 See **Student Dictation,** page 14

34

Name _____

Beginning and Ending l, d, n

LESSON 9

Get Ready

Read the sentences.

   If you are a **duck,** can you swim in a pond? If you are a lion, stay in your **den.** If you are a bird, can you stand on one **leg?** If you are an ant, go to your **nest.**

Get Set

Read the sentences again. Say each word in dark print. Listen for the beginning and the ending sounds.

> The word **duck** begins with the sound for **d.**
>
> The word **den** ends with the sound for **n.** What sound do you hear at the beginning of **den?**
>
> The word **leg** begins with the sound for **l.**
>
> The word **nest** begins with the sound for **n.**

37

Go!

Sounds, Letters, and Words

Print the letter that stands for the missing beginning sound or ending sound. Trace the letters to spell List Words.

LIST WORDS

1. leg
2. dog
3. pen
4. duck
5. nest
6. den

1. dog
2. pen
3. leg
4. den
5. duck
6. nest

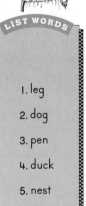 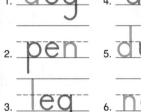

38   Lesson 9 ■ Beginning and Ending l, d, n

Missing Letters

Print the List Words that fit the shapes.

1. l e g   3. d u c k

2. d o g   4. n e s t

Vocabulary

Say the name of each picture. Print the List Word that names each picture.

1. dog   3. duck

2. leg

Rhyming

Print List Words that rhyme with **ten.**

1. pen   2. den

Lesson 9 ▪ Beginning and Ending l, d, n   39

List Words

leg	pen	nest
dog	duck	den

Picture Puzzle

Where are they? Print the List Words that tell where they are.

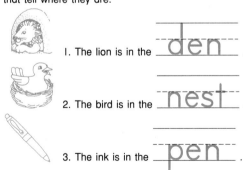

1. The lion is in the **den** .

2. The bird is in the **nest** .

3. The ink is in the **pen** .

Spelling Superstar

Writing

The duck has a special home. Write a sentence that tells about the duck's home.

40   Lesson 9 ▪ Beginning and Ending l, **d, n**

◎ **Spelling Strategy**   To help students recognize beginning and ending *l, d,* or *n,* write the words *face, lip,* and *nose* on the board. Then say *leg* and ask a volunteer to point to the word on the board that has the same beginning letter. Repeat this procedure for beginning *d* and *n* and ending *n,* using these words: for initial *d, dog, cat, fox;* for initial *n, ear, hand, neck;* for final *n, chin, leg, cheek.*

Spelling Superstar   *Page 40*

Offer assistance as needed as students complete the **Writing** activity. Students may want to share their writing by combining all their sentences into a class book called "The Duck in the Nest."

✎ **Writer's Corner** _____

> You may want to share with students books about birds and their homes, such as Ron Hirschi's *What Is a Bird?* and *Where Do Birds Live?* Invite students to write a sentence or two telling the most interesting fact they learned about birds.

Final Test

1. A **duck** says "Quack!"
2. My brother is writing with a red **pen.**
3. The bear slept in its **den.**
4. My **dog** wags her tail when she's happy.
5. Is that **nest** full of baby birds?
6. My left **leg** itches where a bug bit it.

Remind students to check their Final Tests against the List Words and to write any misspelled words in their Spelling Notebook.

★★ All-Star Words

best   luck   log   men

After you write the All-Star Words on the board, pronounce them for the class and discuss their meanings. Then encourage students to work with a partner to write the All-Star Word that rhymes with each word below.

1. truck   (luck)
2. ten   (men)
3. west   (best)
4. fog   (log)

35

Lesson 10

Objective
To spell words with initial or final *w, c,* or *r*

Correlated Phonics Lessons
MCP Phonics, Level A, Lessons 26–28
MCP Discovery Phonics I, If I Could/When It
  Snows/When the Alligator Came to Class
Silver Burdett Ginn *World of Reading,* 1/2, pp. 51, 90

Get Ready   *Page 41*
Read the directions aloud. Then read the sentences
with the class. Ask students what they think might
happen next to the family in the picture.

Get Set
Guide students as they look back at the words in dark
print. Ask the class to say each word with you and to
name the beginning and ending sounds. Then go over
the examples shown with the class.

Pretest
1. Terry's family has a new *car.*
2. Should I open the *can* of beans now?
3. I have a blue *rug* in my room.
4. Use a towel to dry your *wet* hands.
5. I *will* go to the movies tonight.
6. What a *cold* day this is!

Go!   *Pages 42–44*
Read the List Words aloud with students. You may
also want to read the directions aloud at the beginning
of each exercise (**Sounds, Letters, and Words;
Missing Words; Rhyming**) and work through the
first item with the class. As students complete the
exercises, remind them to look back at their
List Words.

 See **Tape Recording,** page 15

Name _____

Beginning and Ending <u>w</u>, <u>c</u>, <u>r</u>

LESSON 10

Get Ready

Read the sentences.

Oh! No! It is a **cold, wet** day.
The **car will** not run.
What **can** we do?
We can walk!

Get Set

Read the sentences again. Say each word
in dark print. Listen for the beginning and
the ending sounds.

> The word **wet** begins with the sound for **w.**
>
> The word **car** begins with the sound for **c.**
> It ends with the sound for **r.** What letter
> stands for the sound at the beginning
> of the word **can?**

41

Go!

Sounds, Letters, and Words
Print the letter that stands for the
missing beginning sound or ending
sound. Trace the letters to spell
List Words.

LIST WORDS

1. car
2. can
3. rug
4. wet
5. will
6. cold

1. wet   4. can
2. will   5. cold
3. rug   6. car

42   Lesson 10 ▪ Beginning and Ending **w, c, r**

36

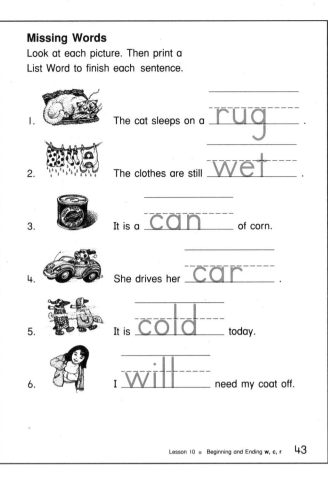

Missing Words

Look at each picture. Then print a
List Word to finish each sentence.

1. The cat sleeps on a __rug__ .

2. The clothes are still __wet__ .

3. It is a __can__ of corn.

4. She drives her __car__ .

5. It is __cold__ today.

6. I __will__ need my coat off.

List Words		
car	rug	will
can	wet	cold

Rhyming

Print the List Word that rhymes with each word given.

1. far __car__

2. hill __will__

3. man __can__

4. told __cold__

5. met __wet__

6. bug __rug__

Spelling Superstar

Writing

The weather map tells about
the weather. Write a sentence
to describe the weather.

⊚ **Spelling Strategy** You may want to call out
each List Word and have the class repeat it and spell
it aloud. As students spell the words, invite them to
stand up and sit down each time they say *w, c,* or *r.*

Spelling Superstar   Page 44

Offer assistance as needed as students complete the
Writing activity. Invite students to share their work by
creating a bulletin board about the weather.

✎ Writer's Corner

> You may want to read the day's weather forecast
> in your local newspaper. Then invite students to
> write about their favorite kind of weather.

Final Test

1. Please buy a **can** of tomatoes at the store.
2. Mother drove her **car** into the garage.
3. Is it too **cold** to play outside?
4. I **will** read this book at home tonight.
5. Let me help you vacuum the **rug.**
6. Your shoes will get **wet** if you step in a puddle.

Remind students to check their Final Tests against
the List Words and to write any misspelled words in
their Spelling Notebook.

★★ All-Star Words

cut   wait   rock   wall

Write the All-Star Words on the board and pronounce
them for the class. Then write the sentences below
on the board. With a partner, students can write the
All-Star Word that completes each sentence.

1. She __(cut)__ the apple into two pieces.
2. Amy can __(wait)__ for the bus at the corner.
3. I found this __(rock)__ out in the yard.
4. Did you hang the picture on the __(wall)__ ?

Lesson 11

Objective
To spell words with initial *v, y, z,* and *qu*

Correlated Phonics Lessons
MCP Phonics, Level A, Lessons 31, 34–35

Get Ready   **Page 45**
Read the directions aloud. Then read the sentences with the class. Invite students to find the queen bee in the picture.

Get Set
Guide students as they look back at the words in dark print. Ask volunteers to say each word and name the beginning sound. Then go over the examples shown with the class.

Pretest
1. We will drive to the park in the *van.*
2. Our class took a trip to the *zoo.*
3. Are *you* working hard?
4. The *queen* sat on her throne.
5. I will *zip* up my jacket.
6. Your dress is *very* pretty.

Go!   **Pages 46–48**
Read the List Words aloud with students. You may also want to read the directions aloud at the beginning of each exercise (**Sounds, Letters, and Words; Vocabulary; Rhyming; Missing Words**) and work through the first item with the class. As students complete the exercises, remind them to look back at their List Words.

For the **Sounds, Letters, and Words** exercise, you might want to point out that the word *zip* imitates the sound it names. Call on several volunteers to say *zip.* Then ask the class what objects might make that sound (a zipper, a car going fast).

 See **Letter Cards,** page 15

38

Beginning v, y, z, qu   **LESSON 11**

Get Ready
Read the sentences.

Can **you** see the **queen** bee? She is **very** big. The other bees **zip** in and out of the hive. They work for the queen bee.

Get Set
Read the sentences again. Say each word in dark print. Listen for the beginning sounds.

 The word **you** begins with the same sound as the word **yo-yo.**

 The word **queen** begins with the sound for **qu.**

 The word **very** begins with the same sound as the word **van.**

 What word begins with the same sound as the word **zoo?**

45

Go!
Sounds, Letters, and Words
Print the letter or letters that stand for the missing beginning sound. Then trace the letters to spell List Words.

LIST WORDS
1. van
2. zoo
3. you
4. queen
5. zip
6. very

1. van   5. you
2. zoo   6. very
3. zip
4. queen

46   Lesson 11 ▪ Beginning v, y, z, qu

Vocabulary

Print a List Word to go with each clue. The List Word begins with the same sound as the picture name.

1. Animals live here. _____ zoo

2. She lives with the king. _____ queen

3. You can ride in this. _____ van

Rhyming

Print a List Word that rhymes with each picture. The word shapes will help you.

1. | v | e | r | y | 2. | z | i | p | 3. | y | o | u |

List Words		
van	you	zip
zoo	queen	very

Missing Words

Look at the picture. Then print List Words to finish the story. The word shapes will help you.

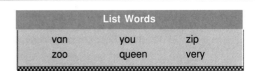

The | q | u | e | e | n | goes out. She rides in

a | v | a | n |. It can | z | i | p | along. She goes

to the | z | o | o |. She sees | v | e | r | y | big

cats. Do | y | o | u | like big cats?

Spelling Superstar

Writing

What would you say if someone gave you a big jar of honey? Write a thank-you note that tells what you would say.

 **Spelling Strategy** Have students say a List Word and then think of another word that begins with the same sound. If students have difficulty thinking of the second word, you might suggest these: *vegetable, visit, vacation, valley; your, year, yellow, yes; zebra, zero; quick, quiet, question.*

Spelling Superstar   *Page 48*

Offer assistance as needed as students complete the **Writing** activity. Students may want to share their writing by using their notes to create a classroom display.

Writer's Corner

You may wish to read a book about insects, such as *Eye Openers: Insects and Crawly Creatures* by Angela Royston. Afterward, invite students to write a sentence that tells the most interesting fact they learned about the bumblebee or another insect.

Final Test

1. Please help me *zip* up my sleeping bag.
2. Thanks *very* much for the gift.
3. We rode in the back of the *van.*
4. What a great time we had at the *zoo!*
5. The *queen* wore a gold crown.
6. Are *you* going to be in the parade?

Remind students to check their Final Tests against the List Words and to write any misspelled words in their Spelling Notebook.

★★ All-Star Words

vest   yes   zebra   quick

With a partner, students can try to guess and write down each All-Star Word as you trace it in the air with your finger. Afterward, write the All-Star Words on the board, pronouncing each one and discussing its meaning. Encourage students to write the words they didn't guess correctly.

Lesson 12

Objective
To spell words that have final *x*, *k*, or *p*

Correlated Phonics Lessons
MCP Phonics, Level A, Lessons 12, 30, 34
MCP Discovery Phonics I, When the Alligator Came to Class/City Rhythms/The Popcorn Popper
Silver Burdett Ginn *World of Reading,* 1/2, p. 99

Get Ready   *Page 49*
Read the directions aloud. Then read the sentences with the class. Ask students whether they would like to try this recipe, and why.

Get Set
Guide students as they look back at the words in dark print. Ask the class to say each word with you and to name the ending sound. Then go over the examples shown with the class.

Pretest
1. Are there **six** boys and seven girls in your class?
2. My crayons are in the blue **box.**
3. Rick climbed to the **top** of the slide.
4. I got a good **book** at the library.
5. When you **mix** red and white, you get pink.
6. Don't **pop** my balloon with that stick!

Go!   *Pages 50–52*
Read the List Words aloud with students. You may also want to read the directions aloud at the beginning of each exercise (**Sounds, Letters, and Words; Rhyming; Puzzle**) and work through the first item with the class. As students complete the exercises, remind them to look back at their List Words.

 See **Rhymes and Songs,** page 14

Get Ready
Read the sentences.

This **book** tells you how to make a good trail snack! You will need:
- **six** large spoons of cereal
- one small **box** of raisins
- three spoons of nuts

Mix in a big bowl. **Pop** some in your mouth!

Get Set
Read the sentences again. Say each word in dark print. Listen for the ending sounds.

 The word **book** ends with the sound for **k.**

 The word **six** ends with the sound for **x.**

What sound do you hear at the end of the word **pop?**

49

Go!
Sounds, Letters, and Words
Print the letter that stands for the missing ending sound. Trace the letters to spell List Words.

LIST WORDS

1. six
2. box
3. top
4. book
5. mix
6. pop

1. pop   4. six
2. mix   5. top
3. book   6. box

50   Lesson 12 ■ Ending x, k, p

40

Rhyming

Read each set of words. Print the two words in each set that rhyme.

six   book   mix

1. six   2. mix

box   pop   top

3. pop   4. top

Say the name of each picture. Print the List Word that rhymes with it.

5. box   6. book

List Words		
six	top	mix
box	book	pop

Puzzle

Print a List Word in the puzzle to name each picture.

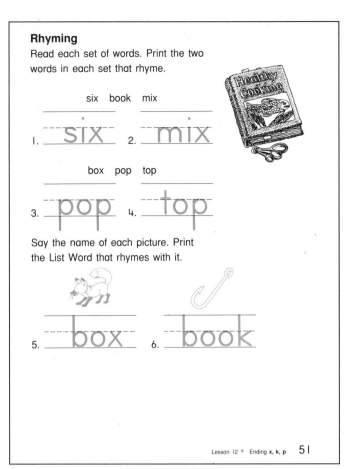

ACROSS

2.

5.

6.

DOWN

1.

3.

4.

Across/Down grid:
- ¹B
- ²B O O K ³S
- X I
- ⁴P ⁵M I X
- ⁶T O P
- P

Spelling Superstar

Writing

The sandwich looks good. Write about how you make your favorite sandwich.

◎ **Spelling Strategy** To give students practice with final *x, k,* and *p,* you might want to say three words ending with *x,* such as *box, fix,* and *tax.* After you ask students what is the same about the words, write them on the board, underlining the *x.* Continue this procedure for words ending with *k* (*work, fork, book*) and with *p* (*map, soap, pop*).

Spelling Superstar   *Page 52*

Offer assistance as needed as students complete the **Writing** activity. Students can share their writing by creating a class book of favorite sandwiches. You may want to photocopy the book so that each student can take a copy home.

✎ Writer's Corner

The class may enjoy preparing food for another class in your school. Select simple recipes from a children's cookbook, such as *Kids Are Natural Cooks* by Roz Ault, or from the class cookbook. Then have students write invitations to send to your guests.

Final Test

1. I like to **mix** peas and carrots.
2. I can read this **book** all by myself.
3. The number **six** looks like an upside-down nine.
4. Is this **box** too small for the present?
5. A pin will **pop** a balloon quickly.
6. I put my name at the **top** of my paper.

Remind students to check their Final Tests against the List Words and to write any misspelled words in their Spelling Notebook.

★★ All-Star Words

ax   fox   bark   step

Write the All-Star Words on the board and pronounce them for the class. Then say the groups of words below. With a partner, students can write the All-Star Word that belongs with each group.

1. dog, wolf, ____(fox)____
2. knife, hatchet, ____(ax)____
3. walk, move, ____(step)____
4. chirp, meow, ____(bark)____

Lesson 13 • Instant Replay

Objective

To review spelling words with beginning and ending *s, t, b, h, m, p, k, j, f, g, l, d, n, w, c, r;* beginning *v, y, z, qu;* ending *x, k, p*

Time Out   *Pages 53–56*

Encourage students to look at the words in their Spelling Notebook. Ask which words in **Lessons 6–12** gave them the most trouble. Write the words on the board and offer assistance for spelling them correctly.

To give students extra help and practice in taking standardized tests, you may want to have them take the Review Test for this lesson on pages 44–45. After scoring the tests, return them to students so that they can record their misspelled words in their Spelling Notebook.

Before students begin each exercise for **Lessons 6–12,** you may want to go over the spelling rule, read the List Words and the directions aloud, and work through the first item with the class.

Take It Home Invite students to collect the List Words in **Lessons 6–12** at home as they read their favorite storybooks or watch their favorite programs. For a complete list of the words, have them take their *Spelling Workout* books home. Students can also use Take It Home Master 1 on pages 46–47 to help them do the activity. Encourage students to bring in their lists to share with the class.

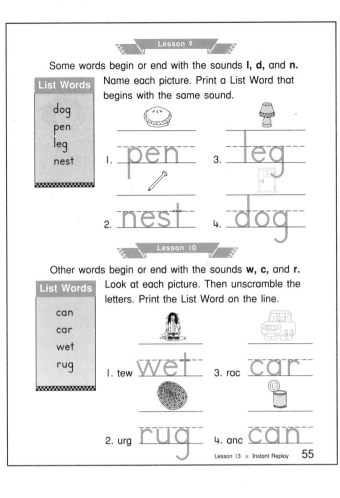

Lesson 9

Some words begin or end with the sounds **l**, **d**, and **n**. Name each picture. Print a List Word that begins with the same sound.

List Words

dog
pen
leg
nest

1. pen
2. nest
3. leg
4. dog

Lesson 10

Other words begin or end with the sounds **w**, **c**, and **r**. Look at each picture. Then unscramble the letters. Print the List Word on the line.

List Words

can
car
wet
rug

1. tew wet
2. urg rug
3. rac car
4. anc can

Lesson 13 ■ Instant Replay   55

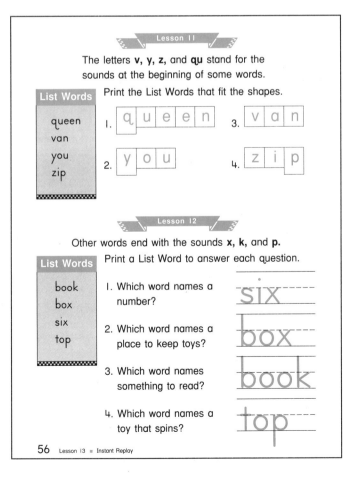

Lesson 11

The letters **v**, **y**, **z**, and **qu** stand for the sounds at the beginning of some words.

List Words

queen
van
you
zip

Print the List Words that fit the shapes.

1. q u e e n
2. y o u
3. v a n
4. z i p

Lesson 12

Other words end with the sounds **x**, **k**, and **p**. Print a List Word to answer each question.

List Words

book
box
six
top

1. Which word names a number? six
2. Which word names a place to keep toys? box
3. Which word names something to read? book
4. Which word names a toy that spins? top

Final Replay Test

1. Please **sit** next to me on the bench.
2. A **map** will help us find our way.
3. Mother opened a new **jar** of olives.
4. Did Peter name his **dog** Jingles?
5. The fresh paint on the door is still **wet.**
6. Does a **queen** rule the country of Denmark?
7. Rosa gave me a spinning **top** for my birthday.
8. She swung the **bat** and hit the baseball.
9. Please hang your coat on the **hook.**
10. We had **fun** playing soccer yesterday.
11. The robins made a **nest** in the maple tree.
12. Uncle Jim drove his **car** to the gas station.
13. My father drives a **van** for a moving company.
14. What an interesting **book** that was!
15. We will ride the **bus** home after school.
16. Look at that kangaroo **hop!**
17. My mother likes to **jog** after work.
18. May I borrow your **pen?**
19. Dave, please open the **can** of tomato sauce.
20. I will send **you** a postcard from Toronto.
21. Each student has a **box** of crayons.
22. Fill the **tub** with hot water.
23. Mrs. Chung wore a gold **pin** on her jacket.
24. Our **pig** won a blue ribbon at the fair.
25. Use glue to fix the broken **leg** on the chair.
26. My grandmother made the **rug** in my bedroom.
27. **Zip** up your coat because it's chilly today.
28. My brother is **six** years old.

Remind students to check their Final Replay Tests against the List Words and to write any misspelled words in their Spelling Notebook.

Spelling Challenge

Encourage groups of students to categorize the words in their Spelling Notebook according to their beginning and ending sounds.

43

Name _____

Instant Replay Test

Side A

Read each set of words. Fill in the circle next to the word that is spelled correctly.

1. (a) hook (c) huke
   (b) hok   (d) huk

2. (a) fune (c) funn
   (b) funne (d) fun

3. (a) neste (c) nest
   (b) nestte (d) nesst

4. (a) lege (c) legg
   (b) legge (d) leg

5. (a) rug   (c) rugg
   (b) ruge (d) rugge

6. (a) kwene (c) quene
   (b) queen (d) quean

7. (a) buk   (c) bokk
   (b) book (d) boke

44

Name _____

Instant Replay Test

Side B

Read each set of words. Fill in the circle
next to the word that is spelled correctly.

8. (a) sitt   (c) siit
   (b) sit   (d) sitte

9. (a) jar   (c) jare
   (b) jarre   (d) jarr

10. (a) buse   (c) bos
    (b) buus   (d) bus

11. (a) boxe   (c) boxx
    (b) boox   (d) box

12. (a) you   (c) yue
    (b) yoo   (d) yooe

13. (a) carre   (c) car
    (b) caar   (d) carr

14. (a) mappe   (c) maap
    (b) mapp   (d) map

15. (a) pinne   (c) piin
    (b) pin   (d) pinn

TAKE IT HOME

Your child has learned to spell many new words and would like to share them with you and your family. Here are some great activities that will help your child review the words in Lessons 6–12 and provide family fun, too!

Look and Listen!

Keep a notebook and a pencil within reach. That way, your child can look and listen for spelling words whenever your family shares a favorite story or program.

bat fun jog map   wet rug up box six
nest car   top queen

Watch Out for Words!

Hey! Who's hogging the road? In the picture, find these things and spell the words that name them:

- things that move on wheels
- a farm animal
- an animal that barks
- a drawing that shows where different places are

- a cozy home for baby birds
- a woman who rules a country
- a thing that covers a floor
- something made of cardboard

What other spelling words can you and your child use to talk about this silly scene?

Lesson 14

Objective

To spell words with initial or medial short *a*

Correlated Phonics Lessons

MCP Phonics, Level A, Lessons 41–44
MCP Discovery Phonics I, When the Alligator Came
  to Class
Silver Burdett Ginn *World of Reading,* 1/2, p. 32

Get Ready   *Page 57*

Read the directions aloud. Then read the poem with
the class. Invite students to identify "the lady"
described in the poem. Encourage students who have
seen the Statue of Liberty to tell what it is like. For
students who are unfamiliar with the statue, discuss
where it is located and its significance.

Get Set

Guide students as they look back at the words in dark
print. Call on volunteers to say each word and name
the sound that *a* stands for. Then go over the
examples shown with the class.

Pretest

1. A firefighter wears a **hat** for protection.
2. Is the **man** who lives next door a plumber?
3. My mother **has** a new dress.
4. The **lamp** in the living room is broken.
5. Jim **and** Sarah live in that house.
6. Hold your brother's **hand** when you cross the road.

Go!   *Pages 58–60*

Read the List Words aloud with students. You may
also want to read the directions aloud at the beginning
of each exercise (**Sounds, Letters, and Words;
Missing Words; Word Groups; Vocabulary**) and
work through the first item with the class. As students
complete the exercises, remind them to look back
at their List Words or in their dictionaries if they
need help.

For the **Sounds, Letters, and Words** exercise,
explain to students that there are three different words
beginning with *h,* and that those answer words can
appear in any order in the *h* answer blanks.

 See **Spelling Aloud,** page 14

48

Short a Sound

LESSON
14

Get Ready

Read the poem.

Who is the lady?
What does she see?
Why is a **lamp** in her **hand?**
She is the one who stands for liberty.
Her light shines over our land.
From the green of the hills,
To the blue of the sea,
Her light is for you **and** for me.

Get Set

Read the poem again. Say each word in
dark print. Listen for the short **a** sounds.

You can hear the short **a** sound in **hand.**
What sound do you hear in the words
lamp and **and?**

57

Go!

Sounds, Letters, and Words

Print the missing letters in each word.
Trace the letters to spell List Words.

1. man   4. and
2. hat   5. hand
3. has   6. lamp

LIST WORDS

1. hat
2. man
3. has
4. lamp
5. and
6. hand

58   Lesson 14 ▪ Short a Sound

Missing Words

Look at each picture. Then print a List Word to finish each sentence.

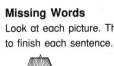 1. Turn on the __lamp__.

2. Vicki __and__ Nancy are sisters.

3. Burt __has__ a new book.

4. Sharon is wearing a pretty __hat__.

Word Groups

Print the List Word that belongs with each group of words.

1. foot, arm, __hand__   3. boy, girl, __man__

2. bed, table, __lamp__   4. dress, shoe, __hat__

List Words		
hat	has	and
man	lamp	hand

Vocabulary

Print the List Word that goes with each clue.

1. owns or holds __has__

2. part of the body __hand__

3. a grown-up boy __man__

4. also or added to __and__

Spelling Superstar

Writing

Many statues show great people. Do you know who this statue shows? Write about this statue or another statue you know.

◎ **Spelling Strategy** To help students recognize the short *a* sound, say each of these words and invite students to choose a List Word or List Words that rhyme with it: *cat, ran, stamp,* and *band.* Then call on volunteers to write each List Word on the board and circle the letter that stands for the short *a* sound. Encourage students to suggest other rhyming words for the List Words.

Spelling Superstar   *Page 60*

Offer assistance as needed as students complete the **Writing** activity. Students may want to share their writing by reading it aloud to the class. Before students begin to read, encourage them to mimic their statues.

✎ Writer's Corner

> The class might enjoy finding out more about the Statue of Liberty by writing to Superintendent Ann Belkov, Statue of Liberty, Ellis Island, NY 10004.

Final Test

1. You **and** I are good friends.
2. The **man** who works in the store is my uncle.
3. Hold the pencil in your **hand.**
4. Where is my straw **hat?**
5. Turn off the **lamp** before you go to sleep.
6. What big ears that elephant **has!**

Remind students to check their Final Tests against the List Words and to write any misspelled words in their Spelling Notebook.

★★ All-Star Words

cat   ran   mask   stand

After you write the All-Star Words on the board, pronounce them for the class and discuss their meanings. Then have students work with a partner to write a sentence for each word. Afterward, ask students to read their sentences aloud.

Lesson 15

Objective
To spell words that have the short *i* sound spelled with *i*

Correlated Phonics Lessons
MCP Phonics, Level A, Lessons 46–49
MCP Discovery Phonics I, City Rhythms
Silver Burdett Ginn *World of Reading,* 1/3, pp. 182–183

Get Ready   *Page 61*
Read the directions aloud. Then read the sentences with the class. Ask students how they think the girl felt when she hit a home run.

Get Set
Guide students as they look back at the words in dark print. Ask volunteers to say each word and name the sound that *i* stands for. Then go over the examples shown with the class.

Pretest
1. Who *hit* that home run?
2. A Great Dane is a *big* dog.
3. The fastest runner will *win* the prize.
4. Let's *fill* the pail with water.
5. *This* kitten is so cute!
6. Jack *did* the dishes.

Go!   *Pages 62–64*
Read the List Words aloud with students. You may also want to read the directions aloud at the beginning of each exercise (**Sounds, Letters, and Words; Missing Words; ABC Order; Rhyming Words**) and work through the first item with the class. As students complete the exercises, remind them to look back at their List Words or in their dictionaries if they need help.

For the **Rhyming Words** exercise, point out to students that the answer to number 2 must begin with a capital letter.

 See **Charades/Pantomime,** page 15

50

Short i Sound

Get Ready
Read the sentences.

Did you ever **hit** the ball and **win** the game? **This** girl **did.** It was the **big** game. The score was tied. The bases were loaded. She stepped up to the plate. She swung the bat and hit the ball. It was a home run!

Get Set
Read the sentences again. Say each word in dark print. Listen for the short **i** sound.

 You can hear the short **i** sound in **hit.** What sound do you hear in the words **win, this, did,** and **big?**

61

Go!
Sounds, Letters, and Words
Print an **i** in each word. Trace the letters to spell List Words.

1. big   5. hit
2. did   6. win
3. this
4. fill

LIST WORDS

1. hit
2. big
3. win
4. fill
5. this
6. did

62   Lesson 15 ■ Short i Sound

Missing Words

Print a List Word to answer each question.
The word shapes will help you.

1. Will you do your homework? I [d i d] it.

2. Why are you in the race? I want to [w i n] .

3. What do you do with the bat? I [h i t] the ball.

4. Do you want some milk? Yes, you can [f i l l]
my glass.

ABC Order

Print each pair of List Words in ABC order.

big   fill

1. big   fill

win   this

2. this   win

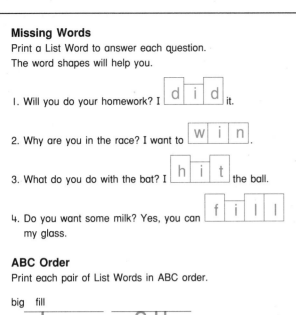

List Words		
hit	win	this
big	fill	did

Rhyming Words

Print the List Word that rhymes with the word in the box.

1. [sit]   Who hit the home run?

2. [lid]   Did you play the game?

3. [miss]   Please wash this cup.

4. [pig]   What a big dog!

Spelling Superstar

Writing

Do you have a favorite game? What
is it called? Write some sentences
that tell how to play the game.

◎ Spelling Strategy   To help students recognize the short *i* sound in the List Words, have them work with a partner and take turns
- writing each word
- saying the word aloud, emphasizing the vowel sound
- pointing to the vowel and naming it.

Spelling Superstar   Page 64
Offer assistance as needed as students complete the **Writing** activity. Students may want to share their writing during playtime by teaching others how to play their game.

✎ Writer's Corner

> You might want to invite older students in your school to speak to your class about a particular sport. Have groups of students prepare questions to ask the guest speakers when they visit.

Final Test
1. We can *win* if we try hard.
2. *Hit* the tennis ball with a racquet.
3. I will *fill* my glass with water.
4. *Did* Jan see me at the fair?
5. Please take *this* note to Mr. Lee.
6. What a *big* pile of dirt that is!

Remind students to check their Final Tests against the List Words and to write any misspelled words in their Spelling Notebook.

★★ All-Star Words

fish   kick   pill   grin

After you write the All-Star Words on the board, pronounce each word and discuss its meaning. Then read the questions below. Invite students to work with a partner to write the All-Star Word that answers each question.

1. What might you do if you are happy?   (grin)
2. What might a doctor give you?   (pill)
3. What lives in water?   (fish)
4. What can you do with your foot?   (kick)

Lesson 16

Objective
To spell words that have medial short *u*

Correlated Phonics Lessons
MCP Phonics, Level A, Lessons 52–55
MCP Discovery Phonics I, Little Bunny's Lunch
Silver Burdett Ginn *World of Reading,* 1/4, pp. 312–313

Get Ready   *Page 65*
Read the directions aloud. Then read the poem with
the class. Invite students to tell why they would or
wouldn't enjoy being a kangaroo.

Get Set
Guide students as they look back at the words in dark
print. Have the class repeat each word after you and
name the sound that *u* stands for. Then go over the
examples shown with the class.

Pretest
1. What a big *hug* Dad gave me!
2. Can you *run* to the fence and back?
3. It's fun to play in the *sun.*
4. Christina can't go, *but* I can.
5. I like to *jump* rope.
6. I have *just* one piece left.

Go!   *Pages 66–68*
Read the List Words aloud with students. You may
also want to read the directions aloud at the beginning
of each exercise (**Sounds, Letters, and Words;
Rhyming; ABC Order; Puzzle**) and work through the
first item with the class. As students complete the
exercises, remind them to look back at their List
Words or in their dictionaries if they need help.

For the **Sounds, Letters, and Words** exercise,
remind students to match letter shapes with the
shapes of the boxes on the page.

 See **Spelling Aloud,** page 14

Short <u>u</u> Sound

LESSON
16

Get Ready

Read the poem.

If I were a kangaroo
I know **just** what I'd do.
I'd bounce around the house a lot
And in the backyard too.
I'd **run** and **jump**
And play all day.
And when the day was through,
I'd wash my face
And paws because
I am a kangaroo.

Get Set

Read the poem again. Say each word in dark
print. Listen for the short **u** sound.

 Listen for the short **u** sound in **jump.**
What sound do you hear in the words **just**
and **run?**

65

Go!

Sounds, Letters, and Words
Print letters to finish each word.
Trace the letters to spell List Words.
The word shapes will help you.

1. s u n   4. h u g

2. j u m p   5. r u n

3. j u s t   6. b u t

LIST WORDS

1. hug
2. run
3. sun
4. but
5. jump
6. just

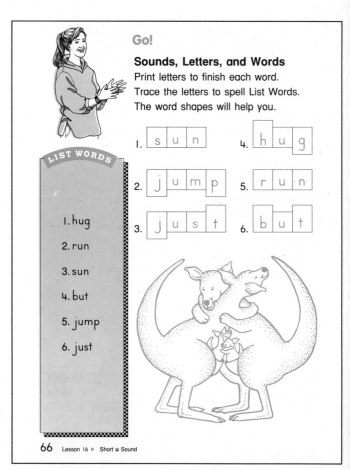

66   Lesson 16 ■ Short **u** Sound

52

Rhyming

Print the List Word that rhymes with each word.

1. bug _hug_   2. pump _jump_

ABC Order

Print each pair of List Words in ABC order.

but   hug

1. _but_   _hug_

sun   jump

2. _jump_   _sun_

just   run

3. _just_   _run_

List Words		
hug	sun	jump
run	but	just

Puzzle

Use List Words to solve the puzzle. Print the letters in the boxes.

ACROSS
2. Kangaroos do this a lot.
3. It shines on the earth.
4. It rhymes with **cut.**

DOWN
1. It means to move in a big hurry.
2. It rhymes with **must.**

Crossword:
- 1 Down / 2 Across: R, J U M P
- 3 Across: S U N
- (down from JUMP): S
- 4 Across: B U T

Spelling Superstar

Writing

What would you do if a kangaroo visited you? Write about how you might show it a good time.

◉ **Spelling Strategy**   To give students practice recognizing the short *u* sound, write these words on the board: *but, jump, mud, has, hug, in, run, on, is, slip, tug, sun, how, wet,* and *just.* Point to each word and have the class
• pronounce the word aloud
• say "short *u* sound" if the word has that sound and "no" if it doesn't.
For each word that has the short *u* sound, call on a volunteer to come to the board and circle the letter that spells the sound.

Spelling Superstar   *Page 68*

Offer assistance as needed as students complete the **Writing** activity. Students may want to share their writing with a partner, who can role-play the kangaroo.

✎ Writer's Corner

Students might enjoy listening as you read one of Jack Kent's stories about a kangaroo named Joey. Invite students to write a few sentences about the part of the story they liked the best.

Final Test

1. That girl can really **run** fast!
2. Can your dog **jump** over this fence?
3. The **sun** will dry the wet clothes quickly.
4. I always get a big **hug** from my sister.
5. I woke up **just** one minute before my brother did.
6. I can come for dinner, **but** I can't sleep over.

Remind students to check their Final Tests against the List Words and to write any misspelled words in their Spelling Notebook.

★★ All-Star Words

mud   hunt   summer   puppet

Write the clues and the All-Star Words on the board in two columns, as shown. With a partner, students can copy what you have written, then draw a line to connect each clue with the correct word.

Clue	All-Star Word
season	mud
wet dirt	hunt
chase	puppet
marionette	summer

Lesson 17

Objective
To spell words with initial or medial short *o*

Correlated Phonics Lessons
MCP Phonics, Level A, Lessons 57–60
MCP Discovery Phonics I, The Popcorn Popper
Silver Burdett Ginn *World of Reading,* 1/3, pp. 202–203

Get Ready   *Page 69*
Read the directions aloud. Then read the sentences
with the class. Invite students to tell what they think
will happen to the carrot. Point out to students that if
they plan to grow a carrot plant, they should ask an
adult to help them with the cutting.

Get Set
Guide students as they look back at the words in dark
print. Call on volunteers to say each word and name
the sound that *o* stands for. Then go over the
examples shown with the class.

Pretest
1. I have a *lot* of friends in my class.
2. Bonnie *got* a basketball for her birthday.
3. It's *not* time to go home yet.
4. Does your uncle have a *job* in an office downtown?
5. Don't *drop* that package!
6. The book fell *off* the table.

Go!   *Pages 70–72*
Read the List Words aloud with students. You may
also want to read the directions aloud at the beginning
of each exercise (**Sounds, Letters, and Words;
Missing Words; Scrambled Letters**) and work
through the first item with the class. As students
complete the exercises, remind them to look back
at their List Words or in their dictionaries if they
need help.

 See **Charades/Pantomime,** page 15

Short o Sound

Get Ready
Read the sentences.

It's a **lot** of fun to grow a
plant. First, get a carrot. Cut **off**
the end. Put it in a small dish.
Pour in water to cover the bottom
of the dish. **Not** too much! Place
the dish in sunlight. Water your
plant when the dish is dry.

Get Set
Read the sentences again. Say each word in
dark print. Listen for the short **o** sound.

 You can hear the short **o** sound in **off.** What
sound do you hear in the words **lot** and **not?**

69

Go!
Sounds, Letters, and Words
Print the missing letters for each word.
Trace the letters to spell List Words.

1. drop   4. not
2. off   5. got
3. lot   6. job

LIST WORDS

1. lot
2. got
3. not
4. job
5. drop
6. off

70   Lesson 17 ■ Short o Sound

54

Missing Words

Look at each picture. Then print a List Word to finish each sentence.

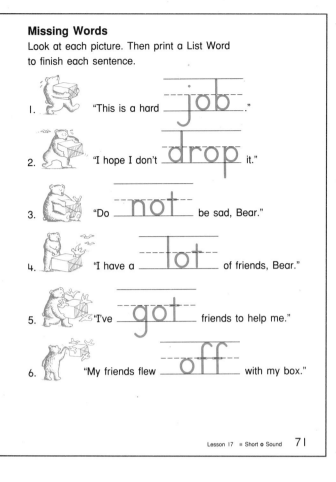

1. "This is a hard **job**."

2. "I hope I don't **drop** it."

3. "Do **not** be sad, Bear."

4. "I have a **lot** of friends, Bear."

5. "I've **got** friends to help me."

6. "My friends flew **off** with my box."

List Words		
lot	not	drop
got	job	off

Scrambled Letters

Unscramble the letters to spell List Words. Print the words on the lines.

1. ffo **off**

2. ton **not**

3. jbo **job**

4. otl **lot**

5. tog **got**

6. ropd **drop**

Spelling Superstar

Writing

Plants need care. Write about how you would take care of a plant.

Spelling Strategy   Write each List Word on the board, leaving a blank for the *o*. Then ask the class to name the missing letter and the vowel sound it stands for. Call on a volunteer to fill in the missing letter and say the complete word.

Spelling Superstar   *Page 72*

Offer assistance as needed as students complete the **Writing** activity. Students may want to share their writing by making a class poster about plant care.

✍ Writer's Corner

> You might want to purchase a houseplant for your classroom and read students the instructions for its care, or follow the directions in the selection and grow a carrot plant. Invite groups of students to make a log and record the plant's progress over several weeks.

Final Test

1. We are ***not*** going to the movies today.
2. Do a ***lot*** of squirrels live in the park?
3. Writing for a newspaper is an interesting ***job.***
4. Watch out or you'll ***drop*** that plate!
5. We stopped at the store and ***got*** a loaf of bread.
6. Take your muddy shoes ***off*** before you come in.

Remind students to check their Final Tests against the List Words and to write any misspelled words in their Spelling Notebook.

★★ All-Star Words

pot   lock   follow   pond

With a partner, students can try to guess and write each All-Star Word as you trace it in the air with your finger. Afterward, write the All-Star Words on the board, pronouncing each one and discussing its meaning. Encourage students to write the words that they didn't guess correctly.

Lesson 18

Objective
To spell words that have the short *e* sound spelled with *e*

Correlated Phonics Lessons
MCP Phonics, Level A, Lessons 63–66
MCP Discovery Phonics I, Best Friends
Silver Burdett Ginn *World of Reading,* 1/2, pp. 86–87

Get Ready   *Page 73*
Read the directions aloud. Then read the riddle with the class. Invite students to try to guess the answer before they turn their books upside-down and look at it.

Get Set
Guide students as they look back at the words in dark print. Have the class repeat each word after you and name the sound that *e* stands for. Then go over the examples shown with the class.

Pretest
1. Vanessa counted *ten* hens.
2. My favorite color is *red.*
3. The *jet* zoomed by in the sky.
4. We *went* to the circus yesterday.
5. What will happen at the *end* of the story?
6. Let's stop and *rest* for a while.

Go!   *Pages 74–76*
Read the List Words aloud with students. You may also want to read the directions aloud at the beginning of each exercise (**Sounds, Letters, and Words; Missing Words; Word Clues; Puzzle**) and work through the first item with the class. As students complete the exercises, remind them to look back at their List Words or in their dictionaries if they need help.

For the **Missing Words** exercise, point out to students that the first word of the story begins with a capital letter *(Ten).*

 See **Tape Recording,** page 15

Name _____

Short e Sound

Get Ready

Read the riddle.

One hen is in the barnyard.
Two hens **rest** on a stoop.
Three hens **went** off to wander.
Ten hens are in the coop.
If you add them up
  before the sun comes up,
  how many hens will crow?

None. Only roosters crow.

Get Set

Read the riddle again. Say each word in dark print. Listen for the short **e** sound.

> **10** You can hear the short **e** sound in **ten.** What vowel sound do you hear in the words **rest** and **went?**

73

Go!

Sounds, Letters, and Words
Print an **e** in each word. Trace the letters to spell List Words.

1. end   4. jet
2. went   5. red
3. rest   6. ten

LIST WORDS

1. ten
2. red
3. jet
4. went
5. end
6. rest

74   Lesson 18 ▪ Short e Sound

56

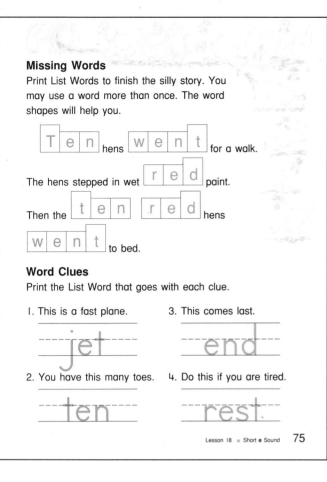

Missing Words

Print List Words to finish the silly story. You may use a word more than once. The word shapes will help you.

T e n hens w e n t for a walk.

The hens stepped in wet r e d paint.

Then the t e n r e d hens

w e n t to bed.

Word Clues

Print the List Word that goes with each clue.

1. This is a fast plane.

jet

3. This comes last.

end

2. You have this many toes.

ten

4. Do this if you are tired.

rest

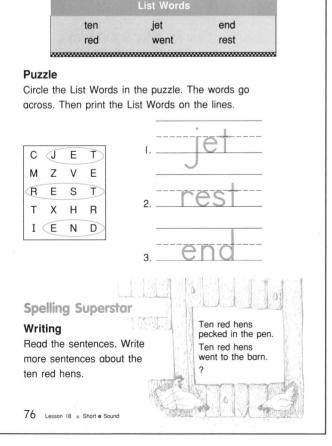

List Words		
ten	jet	end
red	went	rest

Puzzle

Circle the List Words in the puzzle. The words go across. Then print the List Words on the lines.

C	J	E	T
M	Z	V	E
R	E	S	T
T	X	H	R
I	E	N	D

1. jet

2. rest

3. end

Spelling Superstar

Writing

Read the sentences. Write more sentences about the ten red hens.

Ten red hens pecked in the pen.

Ten red hens went to the barn.

?

⊚ Spelling Strategy

Say these words aloud as you write them on the board, leaving blanks for the vowels: *went, ten, end, hum, pit, jet, not, red, ham, rest.* Ask students to tell you which words have the short *e* vowel sound, and write *e* in those words. Erase the words that do not contain the short *e* sound.

Spelling Superstar   *Page 76*

Offer assistance as needed as students complete the **Writing** activity. Students may want to share their writing by reading their sentences to the class.

✎ Writer's Corner

Students might enjoy listening to riddles, such as those in *The Riddle Book* by Roy McKie. Invite students to write their favorite riddle in the book, draw a picture to go with it, and share it with a partner.

Final Test

1. Captain Martinez will fly the ***jet.***
2. Brooke ***went*** home early today.
3. I held one ***end*** of the jump rope.
4. It feels good to ***rest*** after working hard.
5. Are there ***ten*** fish in the tank?
6. Look at that bright ***red*** car!

Remind students to check their Final Tests against the List Words and to write any misspelled words in their Spelling Notebook.

★★ All-Star Words

seven   fence   neck   cent

Scramble the All-Star Words and write them on the board: *ensev, efenc, ckne, tcen.* Invite students to work with a partner to unscramble each word. Afterward, ask volunteers to write the unscrambled words on the board. Pronounce each word and discuss its meaning with the class.

Lesson 19 • Instant Replay

Objective

To review spelling words with the short *a, i, u, o,* and *e* sounds

Time Out   ***Pages 77–80***

Encourage students to look at the words in their Spelling Notebook. Ask which words in **Lessons 14–18** gave them the most trouble. Write the words on the board and offer assistance for spelling them correctly.

To give students extra help and practice in taking standardized tests, you may want to have them take the Review Test for this lesson on pages 60–61. After scoring the tests, return them to students so that they can record their misspelled words in their Spelling Notebook.

Before students begin each exercise for **Lessons 14–18,** you may want to go over the spelling rule, read the List Words and the directions aloud, and work through the first item with the class.

Take It Home   Invite students to listen for, find, and use the List Words in **Lessons 14–18** at home. Suggest that they ask family members to use the words in an after-dinner conversation and to point out List Words that they see on containers or in cookbooks. For a complete list of the words, have students take their *Spelling Workout* books home. Students can also use Take It Home Master 2 on pages 62–63 to help them do the activity. Encourage students to share their lists with the class and to discuss which words were the most difficult to use or find.

58

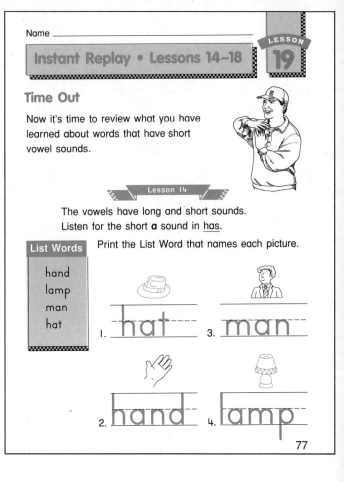

Name _____

Instant Replay • Lessons 14–18   LESSON 19

Time Out

Now it's time to review what you have learned about words that have short vowel sounds.

Lesson 14

The vowels have long and short sounds.
Listen for the short **a** sound in has.

List Words
hand
lamp
man
hat

Print the List Word that names each picture.

1. hat   3. man
2. hand   4. lamp

77

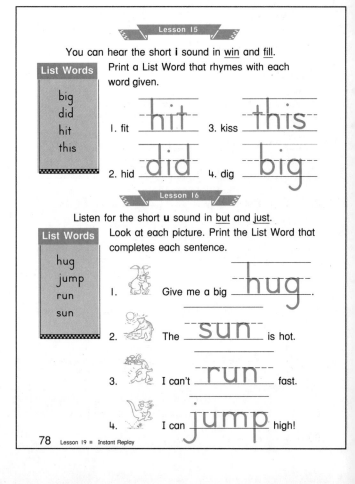

Lesson 15

You can hear the short **i** sound in win and fill.

List Words
big
did
hit
this

Print a List Word that rhymes with each word given.

1. fit — hit   3. kiss — this
2. hid — did   4. dig — big

Lesson 16

Listen for the short **u** sound in but and just.

List Words
hug
jump
run
sun

Look at each picture. Print the List Word that completes each sentence.

1. Give me a big hug
2. The sun is hot.
3. I can't run fast.
4. I can jump high!

78   Lesson 19 ■ Instant Replay

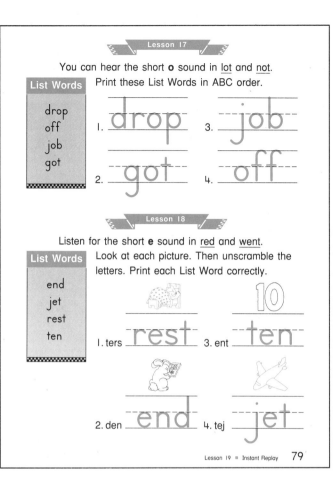

Lesson 17

You can hear the short **o** sound in lot and not.
Print these List Words in ABC order.

List Words

drop
off
job
got

1. drop
2. got
3. job
4. off

Lesson 18

Listen for the short **e** sound in red and went.

List Words

end
jet
rest
ten

Look at each picture. Then unscramble the
letters. Print each List Word correctly.

1. ters   rest
2. den   end
3. ent   ten
4. tej   jet

Lesson 19 ■ Instant Replay   79

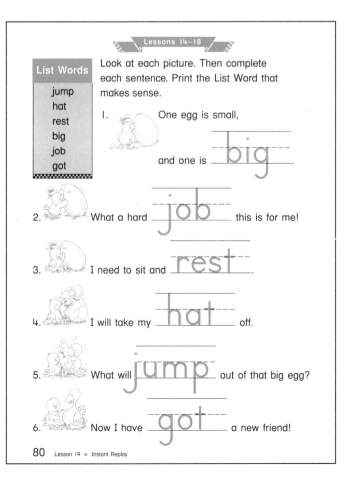

Lessons 14–18

List Words

jump
hat
rest
big
job
got

Look at each picture. Then complete
each sentence. Print the List Word that
makes sense.

1. One egg is small,
   and one is _____ big .

2. What a hard _____ job _____ this is for me!

3. I need to sit and _____ rest _____ .

4. I will take my _____ hat _____ off.

5. What will _____ jump _____ out of that big egg?

6. Now I have _____ got _____ a new friend!

Final Replay Test   *Page 80*

1. A *man* who lives on my street collects rare coins.
2. Did Jennifer *hit* the ball over the fence?
3. Let's *jump* on the trampoline!
4. My grandfather has a *job* at the science museum.
5. We flew to Florida in a big *jet.*
6. Raise your *hand* if you know the answer.
7. What a *big* surprise it is to see you here!
8. Mom gave me a *hug* before I left for school.
9. Carry the vase carefully or you may *drop* it.
10. After the long hike, we needed to *rest.*
11. The *lamp* needs a new light bulb.
12. The ballerina *did* a difficult dance.
13. I wake up when the *sun* rises.
14. Will you wash the dirt *off* my bicycle?
15. A dime is equal to *ten* pennies.
16. I knitted a warm woolen *hat* for myself.
17. Is *this* your favorite book?
18. My older brother will *run* in the race.
19. We stopped at the store and *got* a loaf of bread.
20. This is the *end* of the spelling test.

Remind students to check their Final Replay Tests
against the List Words and to write any misspelled
words in their Spelling Notebook.

Spelling Challenge

After students write the words in their Spelling
Notebook, encourage them to work with a partner to
point to and pronounce the vowel in each word, then
say the complete word.

Name _____

Instant Replay Test

Side A

Read each set of words. Fill in the circle next to the word that is spelled correctly.

1. (a) didde   (c) did
   (b) diid   (d) didd

2. (a) sun   (c) sunn
   (b) sune   (d) sunne

3. (a) haat   (c) hatt
   (b) hat   (d) hatte

4. (a) durp   (c) drupp
   (b) dropp   (d) drop

5. (a) jobb   (c) job
   (b) jobe   (d) jobbe

6. (a) lamp   (c) lammp
   (b) laamp   (d) lam

7. (a) ennd   (c) ende
   (b) end   (d) endd

Instant Replay Test

Side B

Read each set of words. Fill in the circle next to the word that is spelled correctly.

8.   ⓐ reste   ⓒ resst
      ⓑ restte   ⓓ rest

9.   ⓐ hand   ⓒ hannd
      ⓑ hande   ⓓ hend

10. ⓐ hug   ⓒ hugg
      ⓑ huug   ⓓ hugge

11. ⓐ thise   ⓒ thes
      ⓑ thiss   ⓓ this

12. ⓐ jomp   ⓒ jumpe
      ⓑ jumpp   ⓓ jump

13. ⓐ bigg   ⓒ big
      ⓑ bige   ⓓ bigge

14. ⓐ got   ⓒ gotte
      ⓑ gott   ⓓ git

15. ⓐ jett   ⓒ jeet
      ⓑ jit   ⓓ jet

2

TAKE IT HOME

Your child has learned to spell many new words in Lessons 14–18 and would enjoy sharing them with you and your family. Here are some wonderful ideas that will make reviewing those words fun for the whole family.

Table Talk!

Dish up some after-dinner fun for the whole family. Here's how. Have everyone take turns using a spelling word in conversation or finding it on a container or in a cookbook in your kitchen. Encourage your child to jot down all the words that are used or found.

Scrambled Words

Uh-oh! Somebody's stirred up the alphabet soup! Draw a line from each bowl of scrambled letters to the bowl with the correct spelling. Then, you and your child can mix up some spelling scrambles of your own.

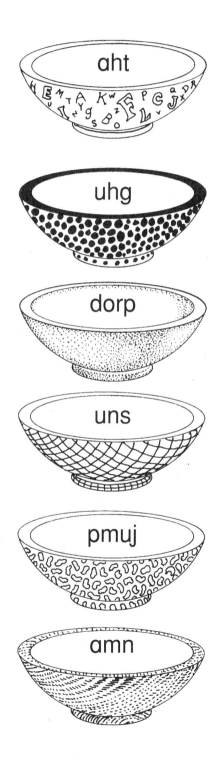

Lesson 20

Objective
To spell words that have the long *a* sound spelled with *a-e*

Correlated Phonics Lessons
MCP Phonics, Level A, Lessons 69–75
MCP Discovery Phonics I, The Baby Who Got All the Blame
Silver Burdett Ginn *World of Reading*, 1/4, p. 367

Get Ready   *Page 81*
Read the directions aloud. Then read the sentences with the class. Encourage students to tell you what part they liked the best.

Get Set
Guide students as they look back at the words in dark print. Ask volunteers to say each word and name the vowel sound they hear. Then go over the examples shown with the class.

Pretest
1. Dad and I will *make* dinner.
2. My cousin *came* to visit.
3. Grandmother *gave* me a new toy.
4. What is your last *name?*
5. *Take* your lunch with you to school.
6. How fun it is to play this *game!*
7. Can you find a *place* to sit?
8. I like to *bake* banana bread.

Go!   *Pages 82–84*
Read the List Words aloud with students. You may also want to read the directions aloud at the beginning of each exercise (**Sounds, Letters, and Words; Puzzle; ABC Order; Rhyming**) and work through the first item with the class. As students complete the exercises, remind them to look back at their List Words or in their dictionaries if they need help.

 See **Student Dictation,** page 14

64

Long *a* Sound

Get Ready

Read the sentences.

Her **name** is Bitsy. She is a baby elephant. Bitsy lives with a circus. When she is happy, she will **make** a noise with her trunk. It sounds like a trumpet! Bitsy played a **game** with the children who **came** to see her. She tickled them with her trunk. This made Bitsy happy and she made her trumpet sound!

Get Set

Read the sentences again. Say each word in dark print. Listen for the long **a** sound.

 You can hear the long **a** sound in **game.** What sound do you hear in the words **name, make,** and **came?**

81

LIST WORDS

1. make
2. came
3. gave
4. name
5. take
6. game
7. place
8. bake

Go!

Sounds, Letters, and Words
Print the missing letters in the words. Trace the letters to spell List Words.

1. gave   5. bake
2. came   6. name
3. place   7. game
4. take   8. make

82   Lesson 20 ■ Long a Sound

Puzzle

Circle each List Word in the puzzle. The word can go across or up and down. Then print the List Words on the lines.

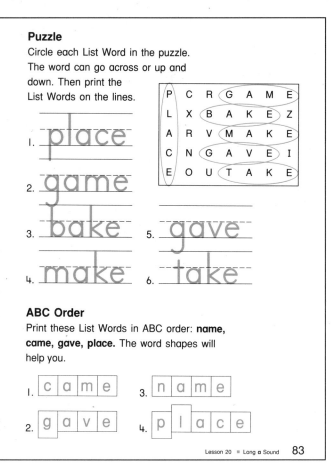

1. place
2. game
3. bake
4. make
5. gave
6. take

ABC Order

Print these List Words in ABC order: **name, came, gave, place.** The word shapes will help you.

1. `c a m e`
2. `g a v e`
3. `n a m e`
4. `p l a c e`

List Words			
make	gave	take	place
came	name	game	bake

Rhyming

Print the List Words that rhyme with **same.**

1. came
2. name
3. game

Print the List Words that rhyme with **lake.**

4. make
5. take
6. bake

Spelling Superstar

Writing

Do you like elephants? Tell about an elephant you have seen at the circus or the zoo.

◉ **Spelling Strategy**   To help students spell the long *a* sound with *a-e*, write these sentences on the board: *Tk the note I gv you to our secret plc. Mk sure no one sees you.* Read the sentences aloud—but circle the incomplete List Words instead of saying them. Then have students write the sentences, adding the missing letters. Supply a clue by telling students that the incomplete words have the long *a* sound.

Spelling Superstar   *Page 84*

Offer assistance as needed as students complete the **Writing** activity. By cutting an elephant shape out of construction paper and gluing their writing onto it, students can share their work with one another. Tape the shapes along a wall to form a parade of elephants.

✎ Writer's Corner _____

Students might enjoy learning more about elephants by writing to the African Wildlife Foundation, 1717 Massachusetts Avenue NW, Suite 602, Washington, DC 20036. The class should write its request on a postcard and specifically request elephant information.

Final Test

1. Do you know the rules of the **game?**
2. My sister's **name** is Tanya.
3. I need a quiet **place** where I can read.
4. My cousin **gave** me his old skates.
5. Adam and Nico **came** into the kitchen.
6. Which model airplane will she **make?**
7. You **bake** the best muffins in the world!
8. Please **take** this book back to the library.

Remind students to check their Final Tests against the List Words and to write any misspelled words in their Spelling Notebook.

★★ All-Star Words

paste   age   tame   late

Write the All-Star Words on the board in the order given. Pronounce them for the class and discuss their meanings. Then encourage students to work with a partner to list the words in ABC order. Afterward, ask volunteers to read their lists.

Lesson 21

Objective
To spell words that have the long *i* sound spelled with *i-e*

Correlated Phonics Lessons
MCP Phonics, Level A, Lessons 76–80
MCP Discovery Phonics I, If I Could
Silver Burdett Ginn *World of Reading,* 1/4, p. 399

Get Ready
Page 85

Read the directions aloud. Then read the poem with the class. Invite students to tell you what is happening in the picture.

Get Set
Guide students as they look back at the words in dark print. Have the class repeat each word after you and name the vowel sound they hear. Then go over the examples shown with the class.

Pretest
1. Lee has *five* sisters.
2. Is this scarf *mine?*
3. I *like* arithmetic.
4. What a bumpy *ride* we had!
5. Is it *time* for art class?
6. Watch how high this *kite* can go!
7. I have a shiny red *bike.*
8. Megan put the *dime* in her bank.

Go!
Pages 86–88

Read the List Words aloud with students. You may also want to read the directions aloud at the beginning of each exercise (**Sounds, Letters, and Words; Missing Words; Vocabulary; Proofreading**) and work through the first item with the class. As students complete the exercises, remind them to look back at their List Words or in their dictionaries if they need help.

 See **Picture Clues,** page 15

Long i Sound

LESSON
21

Get Ready

Read the poem.

I **like** to read.
I like to write.
I like to fly a **kite.**
I like to swim.
I like to hike.
I like to **ride** my **bike.**
When I am sad,
To make me glad,
I think of things I like.

Get Set

Read the poem again. Say each word in dark print. Listen for the long **i** sound.

You can hear the long **i** sound in **kite.**
What sound do you hear in the words **like,**
ride, and **bike?**

85

Go!

Sounds, Letters, and Words
Print the missing **i** and **e** in each word.
Trace the letters to spell List Words.

1. like   5. dime
2. ride   6. kite
3. five   7. bike
4. mine   8. time

LIST WORDS

1. five
2. mine
3. like
4. ride
5. time
6. kite
7. bike
8. dime

86   Lesson 21 ■ Long i Sound

Missing Words

Print List Words to finish the story.
The word shapes will help you.

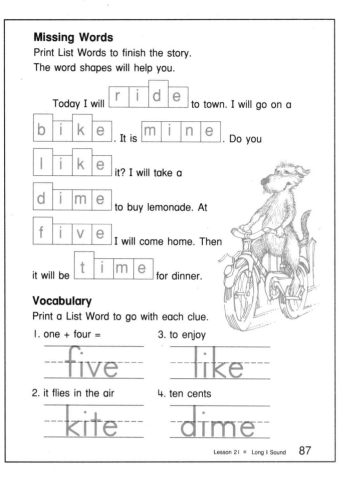

Today I will `r i d e` to town. I will go on a

`b i k e`. It is `m i n e`. Do you

`l i k e` it? I will take a

`d i m e` to buy lemonade. At

`f i v e` I will come home. Then

it will be `t i m e` for dinner.

Vocabulary

Print a List Word to go with each clue.

1. one + four =

five

2. it flies in the air

kite

3. to enjoy

like

4. ten cents

dime

List Words			
five	like	time	bike
mine	ride	kite	dime

Proofreading

Each sentence has a List Word that
is spelled wrong. Circle each one.
Print each word correctly on the line.

Proofreading Marks
⬭ spelling mistake

1. I go to the park
on a (bik.)

bike

2. I (riad) the
ponies there.

ride

3. See the blue (kyte.)

kite

4. It looks like (min.)

mine

5. Soon it is (tiem)
to go home.

time

Spelling Superstar

Writing

Do you like reading, painting, or
playing a game? Write about
what you like to do.

 Spelling Strategy   Write the List Words *kite, ride,* and *dime* on the board and have the class pronounce each word, emphasizing the long *i* sound. Then erase the *e*'s. Invite the class to say each word again and ask, "What do you notice about the vowel sound when there is no *e*?" Replace the *e*'s and help students conclude that *i* and *e* must work together to make the long *i* sound in the words.

Spelling Superstar   *Page 88*

Offer assistance as needed as students complete the **Writing** activity. Students may want to share their work by copying what they wrote onto a class mural titled "What We Like to Do."

✎ Writer's Corner

> You may want to invite some second-graders to your classroom to talk about what they like to do. Afterward, students can write sentences on their class mural about what the speakers said.

Final Test

1. You can **ride** with us to the park.
2. The **kite** sailed in the wind.
3. Do you have a nickel for **five** pennies?
4. It is **time** for me to go.
5. I got new safety reflectors for my **bike.**
6. That sweater is **mine.**
7. Luis has a **dime** in his pocket.
8. What color do you **like** best?

Remind students to check their Final Tests against the List Words and to write any misspelled words in their Spelling Notebook.

★★ All-Star Words

pipe   ice   vine   smile

After you write the All-Star Words on the board, pronounce them for the class and discuss their meanings. Then ask students to draw a picture to go with each word. Have students exchange their pictures with a partner and label each other's drawings with the correct All-Star Word.

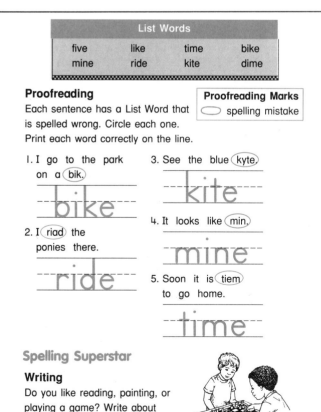

Lesson 22

Objective

To spell words with medial and final long *o*

Correlated Phonics Lessons

MCP Phonics, Level A, Lessons 87–93
MCP Discovery Phonics I, When It Snows
Silver Burdett Ginn *World of Reading,* 1/4, p. 399

Get Ready   *Page 89*

Read the directions aloud. Then read the sentences
with the class. Ask students why they think some
animals have special homes during the winter.

Get Set

Guide students as they look back at the words in dark
print. Call on volunteers to say each word aloud and
name the vowel sound they hear. Then go over the
examples shown with the class.

Pretest

1. I walk *home* after school.
2. The truck rumbled down the *road.*
3. Use *soap* to wash your hands.
4. A *toad* looks very much like a frog.
5. I like *both* dogs and cats.
6. Point your *toe* when you do this dance.
7. Will you help me *fold* the laundry?
8. Tie the package with strong *rope.*

Go!   *Pages 90–92*

Read the List Words aloud with students. You may
also want to read the directions aloud at the beginning
of each exercise (**Sounds, Letters, and Words;
Scrambled Letters; Rhyming; Vocabulary**) and
work through the first item with the class. As
students complete the exercises, remind them to look
back at their List Words or in their dictionaries if they
need help.

For the **Rhyming** exercise, explain to students that
words that rhyme do not always have the same
spelling pattern (*home-comb, toe-go*). After students
complete the exercise, invite them to use a red crayon
to trace the letters that stand for the long *o* sound in
each word.

 See **Variant Spellings,** page 14

Get Ready

Read the sentences.

A bear will spend the winter in a cave.
Most birds will fly south. Where will a **toad**
live when it gets cold? Where will his winter
home be?

In the fall, he will dig a hole
in the mud. He will climb in.
Then he will **fold** leaves over
to cover himself. What will
he do next? He will sleep
until the spring!

Get Set

Read the sentences again. Say each word in
dark print. Listen for the long **o** sound.

 You can hear the long **o** sound in **toad.**
What sound do you hear in the words **home**
and **fold?**

89

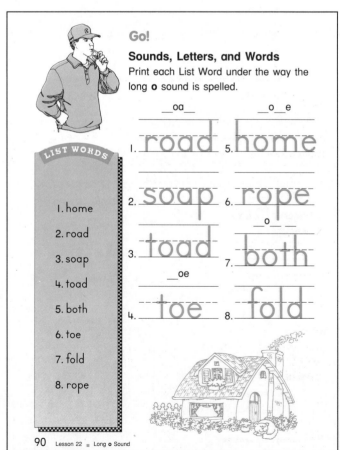

Go!

Sounds, Letters, and Words
Print each List Word under the way the
long **o** sound is spelled.

LIST WORDS

1. home
2. road
3. soap
4. toad
5. both
6. toe
7. fold
8. rope

__oa__

1. road
2. soap
3. toad
4. toe

__o_e

5. home
6. rope
7. both
8. fold

__oe

Scrambled Letters

Unscramble the letters to spell List Words. The word shapes will help you to print the words.

1. odat | t o a d
2. ote | t o e
3. thob | b o t h
4. apos | s o a p
5. dolf | f o l d
6. omeh | h o m e

Rhyming

Print each List Word that rhymes with the word given.

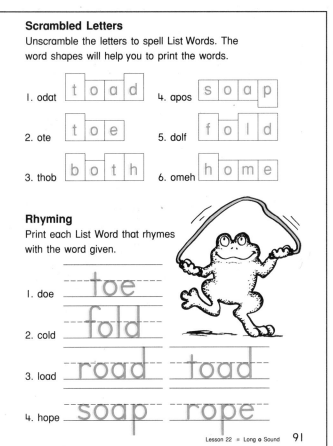

1. doe | toe
2. cold | fold
3. load | road | toad
4. hope | soap | rope

List Words			
home	soap	both	fold
road	toad	toe	rope

Vocabulary

Print a List Word to answer each question.

1. What word means the place where you live?

 home

2. What word means a street?

road

3. What word means the two of you?

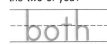 both

Spelling Superstar

Writing

What is winter like where you live? Write some sentences to tell about it.

◎ Spelling Strategy

Write the different ways to spell the long *o* sound on the board as separate column headings: *oa, o-e, o,* and *oe.* Then say each List Word aloud and write it on the board under the correct heading. Have the class repeat the word and name the letter or letters that stand for the long *o* sound.

Spelling Superstar   *Page 92*

Offer assistance as needed as students complete the **Writing** activity. Students may want to share their writing by exchanging sentences with a partner.

✎ Writer's Corner

Keep Looking! by Millicent Selsam and Joyce Hunt explains how various animals spend the winter. You may want to read the book to students and then invite them to write about their favorite part.

Final Test

1. Kick the ball with your ***toe.***
2. Is Kelly's house at the end of the ***road?***
3. Let's ***fold*** this paper to make an airplane.
4. ***Both*** Dan and Ali like to ride bikes.
5. Don't get ***soap*** in your eyes!
6. A little ***toad*** lives in my garden.
7. Use a ***rope*** to pull the wagon.
8. A nest is a bird's ***home.***

Remind students to check their Final Tests against the List Words and to write any misspelled words in their Spelling Notebook.

★★ All-Star Words

bold   doe   coat   tadpole

After you write the All-Star Words on the board, pronounce each one and discuss its meaning. Then say each word below. With a partner, students can write the All-Star Word that has the same beginning sound as the word you say.

1. carry   (coat)
2. table   (tadpole)
3. dance   (doe)
4. butter   (bold)

Lesson 23

Objective

To spell words that have the long *e* sound spelled *e, ea,* and *ee*

Correlated Phonics Lessons

MCP Phonics, Level A, Lessons 94–99
MCP Discovery Phonics I, What Do You See?
Silver Burdett Ginn *World of Reading,* 1/4, p. 367

Get Ready   *Page 93*

Read the directions aloud. Then read the sentences with the class. Ask students what they think would make a good meal for birds.

Get Set

Guide students as they look back at the words in dark print. Have the class repeat each word after you and name the vowel sound they hear. Then go over the examples shown with the class.

Pretest

1. **We** like school.
2. Can we **eat** lunch in the park?
3. What a delicious **meal** that was!
4. The dog chased the squirrel up the **tree.**
5. Max has **three** goldfish.
6. Socks will keep your **feet** warm.
7. Should I **heat** up the soup for lunch?
8. Deena keeps her desk **neat.**

Go!   *Pages 94–96*

Read the List Words aloud with students. You may also want to read the directions aloud at the beginning of each exercise (**Sounds, Letters, and Words; ABC Order; Riddles; Proofreading**) and work through the first item with the class. As students complete the exercises, remind them to look back at their List Words or in their dictionaries if they need help.

 See **Picture Clues,** page 15

Name _____

Long e Sound   LESSON 23

Get Ready

Read the sentences.

   Would you like to see more birds in your yard? If so, feed them! Birds will **eat** lots of foods. Seeds or crumbs make a great bird **meal.** Birds also like apples. Hang an apple from the branch of a **tree.** Try to count how many new birds come to visit!

Get Set

Read the sentences again. Say each word in dark print. Listen for the long **e** sound.

> You can hear the long **e** sound in **tree.** What sound do you hear in the words **eat** and **meal?**

93

Go!

Sounds, Letters, and Words

Print each List Word under the way the long **e** sound is spelled.

e	ea
1. we	5. eat
ee	
2. tree	6. meal
3. three	7. heat
4. feet	8. neat

LIST WORDS

1. we
2. eat
3. meal
4. tree
5. three
6. feet
7. heat
8. neat

94   Lesson 23 ■ Long e Sound

ABC Order

Print each set of List Words in ABC order.

meal   feet   heat

1. feet heat meal

eat   three   neat

2. eat neat three

Riddles

Print a List Word to answer each riddle.
The word shapes will help you.

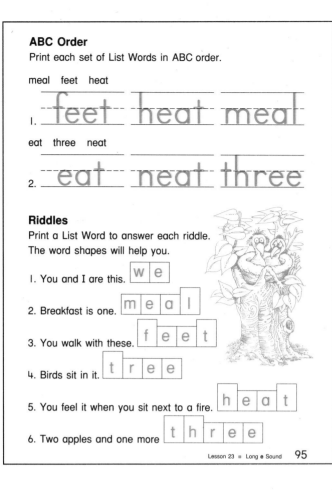

1. You and I are this. | w | e |

2. Breakfast is one. | m | e | a | l |

3. You walk with these. | f | e | e | t |

4. Birds sit in it. | t | r | e | e |

5. You feel it when you sit next to a fire. | h | e | a | t |

6. Two apples and one more | t | h | r | e | e |

Lesson 23 ■ Long e Sound   95

List Words				
we	meal	three	heat
eat	tree	feet	neat

Proofreading

Read the story. Four List Words are
spelled wrong. Circle each one. Then
print each word correctly on the line.

Proofreading Marks
⬭ spelling mistake

My sister and I have a playhouse in
a (tre). (Wie) play games there. We like to
(ete) our lunch there. We keep our
playhouse clean and (neet.)

1. tree   3. eat

2. We 4. neat

Spelling Superstar

Writing

Look at the birds in the tree.
Write a poem about them.
Use List Words in your poem.

96 Lesson 23 ■ Long e Sound

⊙ **Spelling Strategy**   Write these four sets of
words on the board: *hen-he, bed-bee, met-meet,
set-seat.* Read each set aloud and ask the class
• which word in the pair has the long *e* sound
• what letter or letters spell the long *e* sound
• which List Word or List Words spell the long
  e sound the same way.
Ask a volunteer to write the word or words on
the board.

Spelling Superstar   *Page 96*

Offer assistance as needed as students complete the
Writing activity. You might want to record students'
poems as they read them aloud, then play the
recording for another class.

✎ **Writer's Corner** _____

Students might enjoy listening to you read various
poems about birds. Encourage them to write the
title of their favorite poem and to draw a picture to
go with it.

Final Test

1. Is Carlos going to *eat* dinner with us?
2. There is no *heat* in our basement.
3. I got my *feet* wet when I walked in the puddle.
4. Pete's room is always *neat.*
5. Laura gave me *three* green balloons.
6. My favorite *meal* is lunch.
7. Is there an apple *tree* in your yard?
8. What fun *we* had at the park yesterday!

Remind students to check their Final Tests against
the List Words and to write any misspelled words in
their Spelling Notebook.

★★ **All-Star Words**

seal   she   teach   weed

After you write the All-Star Words on the board,
pronounce them for the class and discuss their
meanings. Then hold up a picture of each of these
items: a tree, a seed, a wheel, and a peach. Invite
students to work with a partner to write the All-Star
Word that rhymes with the name of each object
you show (*tree-she, seed-weed, wheel-seal,
peach-teach*).

Lesson 24

Objective

To spell words with the *ou* vowel sound spelled *ou* or *ow*

Get Ready
Page 97

Read the directions aloud. Then read the sentences with the class. Ask students how the scrapbook in the picture was made. What would they put in it if it were theirs?

Get Set

Guide students as they look back at the words in dark print. Ask volunteers to repeat each word after you and to name the vowel sound they hear. Then go over the examples shown with the class.

Pretest

1. Let's go *out* to play.
2. Lewis is *our* friend.
3. The firetruck raced *down* the street.
4. Do you know *how* to ice-skate?
5. I *found* a quarter on the sidewalk.
6. Is Katy's *house* at the end of the road?
7. My pet *mouse* is named Squeaky.
8. I tied a string *around* my finger.

Go!
Pages 98–100

Read the List Words aloud with students, emphasizing the *ou* sound in each word. You may also want to read the directions aloud at the beginning of each exercise (**Sounds, Letters, and Words; Story Puzzle; Puzzle; Missing Words**) and work through the first item with the class. As students complete the exercises, remind them to look back at their List Words or in their dictionaries if they need help.

Before students begin the **Sounds, Letters, and Words** exercise, you may want to write *ou* and *ow* at the top of two columns on the board. Invite students to name words with the *ou* vowel sound and ask them where each word should go. Write each word in the correct column. For the **Story Puzzle** exercise, point out to students that the List Word in the last sentence of the story must begin with a capital letter.

for ESL students See **Rhymes and Songs,** page 14

ou Sound

Get Ready

Read the sentences.

Do you have things you'd like to save? Make a scrapbook. Here's **how.** Look **around** your **house** for pieces of poster board or heavy paper. Cut the pieces into the page size you like. Punch **out** holes at the sides. Tie the pieces together with old shoelaces or string. Then paste the things you want to save on the pages.

Get Set

Read the sentences again. Say each word in dark print. Listen for the **ou** sound.

 You can hear the **ou** sound in **house.** What sound do you hear in the words **how, around,** and **out**?

97

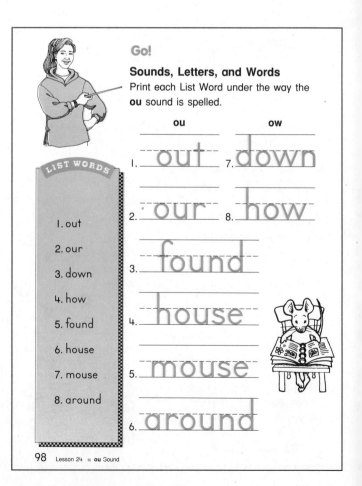

Go!

Sounds, Letters, and Words
Print each List Word under the way the **ou** sound is spelled.

ou	ow
1. out	7. down
2. our	8. how
3. found	
4. house	
5. mouse	
6. around	

LIST WORDS

1. out
2. our
3. down
4. how
5. found
6. house
7. mouse
8. around

98   Lesson 24 ▪ **ou** Sound

Story Puzzle

Print List Words to finish the story.

I have a pet __mouse__ . One day it got

__out__ of the cage. It ran all __around__

the __house__. __How__ can I find it?

Puzzle

Circle each List Word in the puzzle.
Print the List Words on the lines.

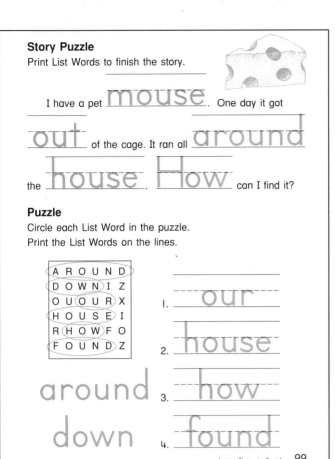

| A R O U N D |
| D O W N I Z |
| O U O U R X |
| H O U S E I |
| R H O W F O |
| F O U N D Z |

1. __our__

2. __house__

3. __how__

4. __found__

List Words

out	down	found	mouse
our	how	house	around

Missing Words

Print a List Word to complete each sentence.
The word shapes will help you.

1. She `f o u n d` the missing book.

2. The ball rolled `d o w n` the hill.

3. The `m o u s e` ran `o u t` the door.

4. Rita and I are doing `o u r` homework.

Spelling Superstar

Writing

People collect stamps, bottle caps, and all kinds of things. What do you collect? Write some sentences to tell about your collection.

◎ **Spelling Strategy**   Write this sentence on the board: *The cow fell on the ground.* Ask students to
• stand up and turn facing away from the board
• listen carefully as you read the sentence
• raise their hands whenever they hear the *ou* sound.
After students are seated again, ask the class to name the words in the sentence that have the *ou* sound. Help students understand that the sound can be spelled two ways: *ow* or *ou*. Then ask volunteers to write List Words on the board in which *ou* spells the *ou* sound. Repeat this procedure for List Words containing *ow*.

Spelling Superstar   *Page 100*

Offer assistance as needed as students complete the **Writing** activity. Students may want to share their writing by bringing in one or more items from their collection and sharing the items and their sentences with the class.

✍ Writer's Corner

Invite students to bring in small rocks, stones, or pebbles to help make a rock-collection display in your classroom. As part of the display, have students write information about the rocks (i.e., where they were found, what they look like) and include a book, such as *Rock Collecting* by Roma Gans.

Final Test

1. I really like *our* new apartment.
2. Watch *out* for bees on those flowers!
3. My brother *found* my lost book.
4. When did you learn *how* to swim?
5. The marbles rolled *down* the stairs.
6. We saw a *mouse* in the barn.
7. I watched the fish swim *around* in the bowl.
8. Is your new *house* near the school?

Remind students to check their Final Tests against the List Words and to write any misspelled words in their Spelling Notebook.

★★ All-Star Words

frown   ouch   ground   owl

After you write the All-Star Words on the board, pronounce them for the class. Then read the sentences below. Students can write the All-Star Word that completes each sentence.

1. When I stubbed my toe, I said, "(Ouch)!"
2. The (owl) caught a mouse.
3. It is better to smile than to (frown).
4. Gophers live under the (ground).

Lesson 25 • Instant Replay

Objective
To review spelling words with the long *a, i, o,* and *e* sounds; and the *ou* sound

Time Out   *Pages 101–104*
Encourage students to look at the words in their Spelling Notebook. Ask which words in **Lessons 20–24** gave them the most trouble. Write the words on the board and offer assistance for spelling them correctly.

To give students extra help and practice in taking standardized tests, you may want to have them take the Review Test for this lesson on pages 76–77. After scoring the tests, return them to students so that they can record their misspelled words in their Spelling Notebook.

Before students begin each exercise for **Lessons 20–24,** you may want to go over the spelling rule, read the List Words and the directions aloud, and work through the first item with the class.

Take It Home Invite students and their families to write down several List Words in **Lessons 20–24.** On their next outing to do errands, suggest that they look for the List Words on signs and containers. For a complete list of the words, have students take their *Spelling Workout* books home. Students can also use Take It Home Master 3 on pages 78–79 to help them do the activity. Encourage students to bring in their lists and to discuss which words they were able to find.

Name _____

Instant Replay • Lessons 20–24   LESSON 25

Time Out
Take another look at words with long vowel sounds and the **ou** sound.

Lesson 20
Sometimes **a** and **e** together in a word make the long **a** sound, as in <u>game</u>.

List Words
make
came
bake
name

Print the List Words that rhyme with each picture's name.

1. make 3. came
2. bake 4. name

101

Lesson 21
Listen for the long **i** sound in <u>ride</u>.

List Words
kite
bike
five
dime

Print the List Word that names each picture.

1. dime 3. bike
2. five 4. kite

Lesson 22
Listen for the long **o** sound in <u>toe</u>, <u>fold</u>, <u>home</u>, and <u>soap</u>.

List Words
fold
rope
road
toe

Print the List Words that rhyme with each picture name.

1. toe 3. road
2. fold 4. rope

102   Lesson 25   Instant Replay

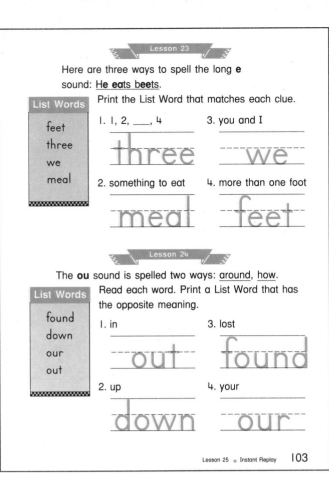

1. Breakfast is a very important *meal.*
2. The newspaper costs a *dime.*
3. Will you show me how to *make* a paper hat?
4. Do not let the gerbil *out* of its cage.
5. My grandparents *came* to this country from China.
6. Can *we* borrow two pencils and some paper?
7. What a bumpy *road* this is!
8. The car can hold *five* people.
9. I can't untie this *rope.*
10. Mark *found* a small blue egg under the bush.
11. Please do not *fold* my drawing in half.
12. The bread must *bake* for one hour.
13. Be careful as you walk *down* the stairs.
14. Is there enough wind to fly a *kite?*
15. I told the story of the *three* little pigs.
16. Write your *name* at the top of the page.
17. My *toe* poked a hole in my sneaker!
18. Will *our* class use the gym today?
19. My sister took the training wheels off the *bike.*
20. The new couch is six *feet* long.

Remind students to check their Final Replay Tests against the List Words and to write any misspelled words in their Spelling Notebook.

Spelling Challenge

Encourage students to work with a partner to circle the vowel or vowels in each word in their Spelling Notebook. Students can then take turns saying each word aloud, emphasizing the vowel sound, and telling whether it is the long *a, i, o,* or *e* sound or the *ou* sound.

Instant Replay Test

Side A

Read each set of words. Fill in the circle
next to the word that is spelled correctly.

1. (a) baik   (c) bak
   (b) backe   (d) bake

2. (a) fiev   (c) fiv
   (b) five   (d) fivv

3. (a) toe   (c) tooe
   (b) tou   (d) toa

4. (a) feete   (c) feit
   (b) feet   (d) fet

5. (a) make   (c) makk
   (b) maik   (d) macke

6. (a) dimme   (c) dime
   (b) diem   (d) dimm

7. (a) oure   (c) ourr
   (b) our   (d) owr

Name _____

Instant Replay Test

Side B

Read each set of words. Fill in the circle next to the word that is spelled correctly.

8.   ⓐ fownd   ⓒ found
       ⓑ founde   ⓓ fonde

9.   ⓐ namme   ⓒ nam
       ⓑ name   ⓓ naim

10. ⓐ thre   ⓒ threa
      ⓑ three   ⓓ thrre

11. ⓐ roap   ⓒ rope
      ⓑ roep   ⓓ roop

12. ⓐ bicke   ⓒ bike
      ⓑ bik   ⓓ biek

13. ⓐ down   ⓒ doen
      ⓑ doun   ⓓ downe

14. ⓐ meal   ⓒ mele
      ⓑ meel   ⓓ meale

15. ⓐ foeld   ⓒ foled
      ⓑ fold   ⓓ folde

TAKE IT HOME

Your child has learned to spell many new words and would like to share them with you and your family. Here are some wonderful ways to help your child review the words in Lessons 20–24 and have fun at the same time!

Shopping for Spelling!

Have your child "go shopping" for spelling words the next time you have errands to run. Encourage your child to carry a list of words, and then locate them on signs and packaging as you go from store to store. Or, for real one-stop shopping, visit a bookstore!

toe down found
feet name bike
make our we
rope
meal dime three
kit
out
fold five
came bake road

Once Upon a Word

With your child, take turns telling a story—the sillier the better! At each turn, take one or more words from the storybook and work them into your tale. For example, you could start off with, "As I walked **down** the **road** one day, guess what I **found**?" Just use the pictures and your own imaginations!

rope
meal
out
found
we
name
came
road
make
fold
feet
dime
bake
kite
toe
our
down
three
bike
five

Lesson 26

Objective
To spell words with initial *r* blends

Correlated Phonics Lessons
MCP Phonics, Level A, Lessons 104–105
MCP Discovery Phonics I, What Do You See?/Who Said Boo?/When the Alligator Came to Class/Best Friends/Little Bunny's Lunch
Silver Burdett Ginn *World of Reading,* 1/4, p. 414

Get Ready   **Page 105**
Read the directions aloud. Then read the sentences with the class. Ask students to suggest answers to the questions before they turn their books upside-down and read the answers.

Get Set
Guide students as they look back at the words in dark print. Ask volunteers to say the words and name the beginning sounds. Then go over the examples shown with the class.

Pretest
1. My dog is *brown* and white.
2. The leaves on the tree are *green.*
3. Don't fall into the *trap!*
4. What city did you come *from?*
5. Brad will *drink* milk with his lunch.
6. The glass *broke* when it fell on the floor.
7. The tadpole will *grow* to be a frog.
8. Does this *train* leave at ten o'clock?

Go!   **Pages 106–108**
Read the List Words aloud with students, helping them emphasize the sounds of the *r* blends. You may also want to read the directions aloud at the beginning of each exercise (**Sounds, Letters, and Words; ABC Order; Missing Words; Rhyming Words**) and work through the first item with the class. As students complete the exercises, remind them to look back at their List Words or in their dictionaries if they need help. For the **Sounds, Letters, and Words** exercise, encourage students to refer to the List Words to help them complete the exercise.

 See **Letter Cards,** page 15

---

r Blends

Get Ready
Read the sentences.

How now **brown** cow? Have you any jokes? No? Well, here are a few you might like:
1. What **drink** do you get when you cross a cow with a jogger?
2. What do you get **from** a cow at the North Pole?
3. Why don't cows tell jokes?

1. a milkshake
2. cold cream
3. They're always in a bad mooood!

Get Set
Read the sentences again. Say each word in dark print. Listen for the beginning sounds.

The word **train** begins with the sounds for **t** and **r**. The letter **r** can form a **blend** when it follows another letter. What **r** blend sounds do you hear at the beginning of the words **brown, drink,** and **from?**

105

Go!
Sounds, Letters, and Words
Print the missing letters in each word.
Trace the letters to spell List Words.

LIST WORDS
1. brown
2. green
3. trap
4. from
5. drink
6. broke
7. grow
8. train

1. from
2. grow
3. brown
4. broke
5. drink
6. green
7. trap
8. train

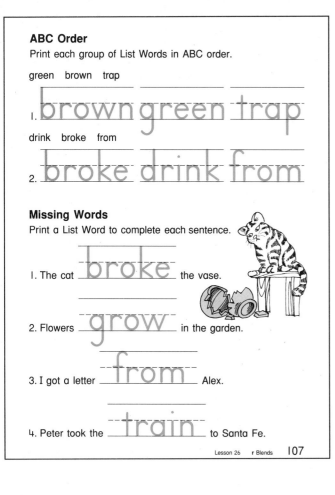

ABC Order
Print each group of List Words in ABC order.

green   brown   trap

1. brown   green   trap

drink   broke   from

2. broke   drink   from

Missing Words
Print a List Word to complete each sentence.

1. The cat broke the vase.

2. Flowers grow in the garden.

3. I got a letter from Alex.

4. Peter took the train to Santa Fe.

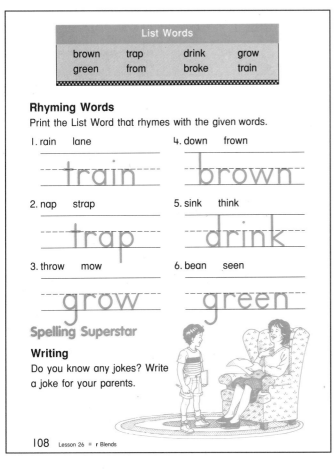

List Words

brown	trap	drink	grow
green	from	broke	train

Rhyming Words
Print the List Word that rhymes with the given words.

1. rain   lane

train

2. nap   strap

trap

3. throw   mow

grow

4. down   frown

brown

5. sink   think

drink

6. bean   seen

green

Spelling Superstar

Writing
Do you know any jokes? Write a joke for your parents.

⊙ Spelling Strategy   Write the word pairs *bag/brag, dot/drop, fog/frog, tip/trip,* and *gate/gray* on the board, each at the top of a column. Use *bag/brag* to illustrate the differences in sound and spelling between words that begin with *b* followed by a vowel and those that begin with the *br* blend. Then circle each *r* blend and ask the class to name a List Word or List Words that begin with the same blend. Write the words on the board in the appropriate columns.

Spelling Superstar   *Page 108*
Offer assistance as needed as students complete the **Writing** activity. Invite students to tell their jokes to the class before they take them home to share with their parents.

✎ Writer's Corner
You may wish to bring in newspaper or magazine comic strips, block out the words in the speech balloons, and photocopy the pages. Distribute the copies and invite students to write their own words in the speech balloons.

Final Test
1. Nicole got a long letter *from* Chris.
2. Is your new coat *brown?*
3. What beautiful flowers *grow* in your garden!
4. Let's glue the vase that you *broke.*
5. Does the *train* have a caboose?
6. I will *drink* my juice with a straw.
7. Many frogs and turtles are *green.*
8. A spider's web is a *trap* for flies.

Remind students to check their Final Tests against the List Words and to write any misspelled words in their Spelling Notebook.

★★ All-Star Words

great   drum   bridge   froze

Write each All-Star Word on the board, pronouncing it for the class and discussing its meaning. Then write the sentences below on the board. With a partner, students can write the All-Star Word that rhymes with each underlined word.

1. I walked along the <u>ridge</u>. (bridge)
2. Did you eat a <u>plum</u>? (drum)
3. I was <u>late</u> for school. (great)
4. What a beautiful <u>rose</u>! (froze)

Lesson 27

Objective
To spell words that have initial *l* blends

Correlated Phonics Lessons
MCP Phonics, Level A, Lessons 106–107
MCP Discovery Phonics I, The Baby Who Got All the Blame/What Do You See?/When the Alligator Came to Class/Best Friends
Silver Burdett Ginn *World of Reading,* 1/4, p. 385

Get Ready   *Page 109*
Read the directions aloud. Then read the sentences with the class. Invite students to tell you what the picture shows and to give the time on the clock.

Get Set
Guide students as they look back at the words in dark print. Ask volunteers to say the words and name the beginning sounds. Then go over the examples shown with the class.

Pretest
1. Am I *glad* to see you!
2. They raise the American *flag* each morning.
3. Can you come out to *play?*
4. I have new *black* shoes.
5. Did that *clock* stop when the power went out?
6. Ricardo made a vase out of *clay.*
7. Amanda's mom will *fly* the plane.
8. The sky is bright *blue* today.

Go!   *Pages 110–112*
Read the List Words aloud with students, helping them emphasize the sounds of the *l* blends. You may also want to read the directions aloud at the beginning of each exercise (**Sounds, Letters, and Words; Beginning Sounds; Vocabulary; Proofreading**) and work through the first item with the class. As students complete the exercises, remind them to look back at their List Words or in their dictionaries if they need help.

 See **Categorizing,** page 15

Name _____

l Blends

Get Ready
Read the sentences.

Brrring! Brrring! The alarm **clock** is ringing. It's time to wake up. What time is it? How do you know?

The little **black** hand is on the eight. The big black hand is on the twelve. Wow! Time flies by quickly! Do you know how the monkey made time really **fly?** He threw the clock out the window!

Get Set
Read the sentences again. Say each word in dark print. Listen for the beginning sounds.

 The word **clock** begins with the sounds for **c** and **l.** The letter **l** can form a **blend** when it follows another letter. What **l** blend sounds do you hear at the beginning of the words **black** and **fly?**

109

Go!

Sounds, Letters, and Words
Print the missing blends for the words. Trace the letters to spell List Words.

LIST WORDS
1. glad
2. flag
3. play
4. black
5. clock
6. clay
7. fly
8. blue

1. flag   5. blue
2. clock   6. play
3. black   7. fly
4. glad   8. clay

Beginning Sounds

Print the List Words that begin with the blends shown.

cl   bl

1. _____   5. _____

2. _____   6. _____

fl   gl

3. _____   7. _____

pl

4. _____

8. _____

Vocabulary

Print a List Word to match each clue.

1. Do this at recess.   3. Make a pot with this.

_____   _____

2. This is the opposite of white.   4. This tells time.

_____   _____

List Words

| glad | play | clock | fly |
| flag | black | clay | blue |

Proofreading

Each sentence has two mistakes. Use the proofreading marks to fix each mistake. Write the misspelled List Words on the lines.

Proofreading Marks
- ⬭ spelling mistake
- ⊙ add period

1. A flagg flies above my school

_____

_____

2. Its colors are red, white, and bloo

_____

_____

3. It makes me gled to see it fli in the wind.

_____ _____

Spelling Superstar

Writing

What is your favorite time of day? Write some sentences that tell what you do at that time.

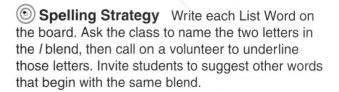

⊚ **Spelling Strategy** Write each List Word on the board. Ask the class to name the two letters in the *l* blend, then call on a volunteer to underline those letters. Invite students to suggest other words that begin with the same blend.

Spelling Superstar   *Page 112*

Offer assistance as needed as students complete the **Writing** activity. Students may want to share their writing by making a bulletin-board display titled "Around the Clock." Students can arrange their sentences in chronological order.

✐ Writer's Corner

Students might enjoy listening to *Nine O'Clock Lullaby* by Marilyn Singer, which tells what is happening at different times in different places around the world. Help students locate the place they liked best on a map and have them write a sentence telling why they like it.

Final Test

1. I was **glad** when it stopped raining.
2. Our car is **black** with a red stripe.
3. What a pretty **blue** dress that is!
4. Did the ticking of the **clock** keep you awake?
5. Let's **play** hide and seek.
6. Is a penguin a bird that cannot **fly?**
7. Blair carried the **flag** in the parade.
8. The dirt in our garden is full of **clay.**

Remind students to check their Final Tests against the List Words and to write any misspelled words in their Spelling Notebook.

★★ All-Star Words

plane   glass   clean   flashlight

Write the clues and the All-Star Words on the board in two columns, as shown below. Partners can copy what you have written, then draw a line to match each clue with the correct word.

Clue	**All-Star Word**
not dirty	plane
it flies	flashlight
used in a window	clean
it lights up	glass

Lesson 28

Objective
To spell words with initial *s* blends or final *st*

Correlated Phonics Lessons
MCP Phonics, Level A, Lessons 108–109
MCP Discovery Phonics I, When It Snows/City Rhythms
Silver Burdett Ginn *World of Reading,* 1/4, pp. 381, 414

Get Ready   **Page 113**
Read the directions aloud. Then read the poem with
the class. Ask volunteers to describe what is
happening in the picture.

Get Set
Guide students as they look back at the words in
dark print. Call on volunteers to say each word and
name the *s* blend. Then go over the examples shown
with the class.

Pretest
1. Our new kitten is very **small.**
2. Friday is the **last** day of the school week.
3. I spilled a **spot** of paint on the floor.
4. Drivers should go **slow** when it rains.
5. Did you have fun playing in the **snow?**
6. Can I have a **spoon** so that I can eat the soup?
7. Please don't **slide** on the slippery floor.
8. What a bright **star** that is!

Go!   **Pages 114–116**
Read the List Words aloud with students. You may
also want to read the directions aloud at the
beginning of each exercise (**Sounds, Letters, and
Words; Missing Words; Rhyming; Missing
Words**) and work through the first item with the
class. As students complete the exercises, remind them to
look back at their List Words or in their dictionaries if
they need help. For the **Sounds, Letters, and
Words** exercise, point out to students that both *sl*
and *sn* are correct answers for numbers 1 and 3.

 See **Rhymes and Songs,** page 14

Name _____

s Blends

LESSON
28

Get Ready
Read the poem.

Whoa!
There they go!
Two feet, one board,
and a big hill of **snow!**
Last ride—no way!
Hey, we could **slide** all day!

Get Set
Read the poem again. Say each word in dark
print. Listen for the **s** blends.

> The word **slide** begins with the sounds for **s**
> and **l.** The letter **s** can form a **blend** when it
> is followed by another letter. What **s** blend
> sound do you hear at the beginning of the
> word **snow?** What **s** blend sound do you hear
> at the end of the word **last?**

113

Go!
Sounds, Letters, and Words
Print the missing letters for the words.
Trace the letters to spell List Words.

LIST WORDS

1. small
2. last
3. spot
4. slow
5. snow
6. spoon
7. slide
8. star

1. slow
2. small
3. snow
4. slide
5. spoon
6. star
7. last
8. spot

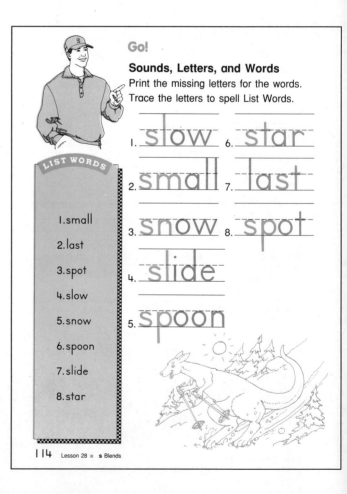

114   Lesson 28 ■ s Blends

Missing Words

Print List Words to complete the sentences. The word shapes will help you.

1. A little dot is a `small` `spot`.

2. Low rhymes with `slow` and `snow`.

3. Eat your soup with a `spoon`.

4. Ride and hide rhyme with `slide`.

5. A `star` shines in the sky.

6. It rained `last` night.

Rhyming

Print the List Word that rhymes with each word given.

1. car   star
2. hot   spot
3. fast   last
4. moon   spoon

List Words			
small	spot	snow	slide
last	slow	spoon	star

Missing Words

Print List Words to finish the story.

I like to play in the 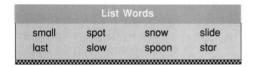snow . I find a

small hill. Then I slide

down it! Sometimes the ride is fast, and sometimes the

ride is 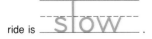slow .

Spelling Superstar

Writing

Some rides are fast. Some are slow. Write some sentences about a ride you like.

⊙ **Spelling Strategy**   Write all the List Words on the board except *last* and read them aloud. As each word is read, ask students what two sounds are heard at the beginning. Write their response on the board. Then write the word *last*. Ask students what two sounds are heard at the end and add their answer to the board. Invite students to suggest additional words that contain initial s blends, final *st*, and other blends they have learned (initial *r* and *l* blends).

Spelling Superstar   *Page 116*

Offer assistance as needed as students complete the **Writing** activity. Students may want to share their writing by reading their sentences aloud.

✐ **Writer's Corner** _____

> You might want to read the class a poem about an activity such as swinging, sledding, or riding in a sleigh. Afterward, encourage students to write a sentence telling how the poem made them feel.

Final Test

1. May I go down the **slide** first?
2. She wore a badge shaped like a **star.**
3. I used a **spoon** to stir the stew.
4. The **snow** looks so white and fluffy!
5. A mouse is a **small** animal.
6. On his **last** birthday, he was seven.
7. Oh, no! I got an ink **spot** on my new shirt!
8. Lullabies are **slow** and quiet songs.

Remind students to check their Final Tests against the List Words and to write any misspelled words in their Spelling Notebook.

★★ All-Star Words

west   stick   sled   speak

Write the All-Star Words on the board and pronounce them for the class. Then read aloud each clue below. With a partner, students can write the All-Star Word that goes with each clue.

1. talk (speak)
2. opposite of east (west)
3. piece of wood (stick)
4. something to ride on (sled)

Lesson 29

Objective

To spell words in which *y* spells the long *i* sound or helps spell the long *a* sound

Correlated Phonics Lessons

MCP Phonics, Level A, Lessons 113–114
Silver Burdett Ginn *World of Reading,* 1/5, pp. 254–255; 1/6, p. 61

Get Ready   *Page 117*

Read the directions aloud. Then read the sentences with the class. Encourage sets of partners to role-play the knock-knock joke in the book as well as other knock-knock jokes they know.

Get Set

Guide students as they look back at the words in dark print. Ask volunteers to say each word and name the sound that *y* spells. Then go over the examples shown with the class, pointing out that the long *a* sound is spelled *ey* in *they.*

Pretest

1. Stay ***away*** from the hot stove.
2. Do you have enough money to ***pay*** for the book?
3. You can do it! ***Try*** again.
4. There are dark clouds in the ***sky.***
5. ***They*** are coming to dinner tonight.
6. The baby will not ***cry*** if you play with her.
7. Have you seen ***my*** hat?
8. There are twenty-four hours in a ***day.***

Go!   *Pages 118–120*

Read the List Words aloud with students. You may also want to read the directions aloud at the beginning of each exercise (**Sounds, Letters, and Words; Opposites; Ending Sounds; Scrambled Letters; Proofreading**) and work through the first item with the class. As students complete the exercises, remind them to look back at their List Words or in their dictionaries if they need help.

 See **Tape Recording,** page 15

y as a Vowel

LESSON 29

Get Ready

Read the sentences.

Hey, hey! What do you say?
I could tell knock-knock jokes all **day!**

Knock. Knock.

Who's there?

Boo.

Boo who?

Try not to **cry.**
Knock. Knock.

Go **away!**

Get Set

Read the sentences again. Say each word in dark print. Listen for the sound the **y** spells in each word.

 The letter **y** spells the long **i** sound in **fly.** You can hear the long **i** sound in **try** and **cry.**

The letter **y** helps to spell the long **a** sound in **tray.** What vowel sound does **y** help to spell in **day** and **away?**

117

Go!

Sounds, Letters, and Words

Print each List Word under its heading.

y helps to spell /ā/	y spells /ī/
1. away	5. try
2. pay	6. sky
3. they	7. cry
4. day	8. my

LIST WORDS

1. away
2. pay
3. try
4. sky
5. they
6. cry
7. my
8. day

Opposites

Print the List Word that means the opposite of each word.

1. here — away
3. laugh — cry
5. night — day
2. we — they
4. your — my
6. earth — sky

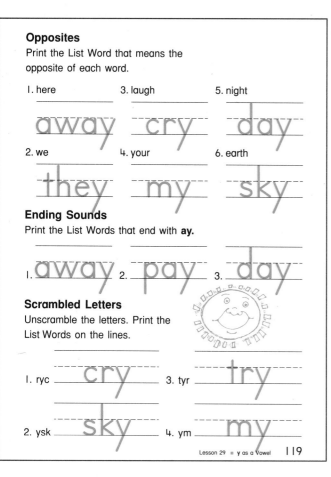

Ending Sounds

Print the List Words that end with **ay.**

1. away
2. pay
3. day

Scrambled Letters

Unscramble the letters. Print the List Words on the lines.

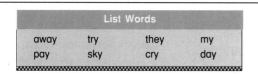

1. ryc — cry
3. tyr — try
2. ysk — sky
4. ym — my

List Words

away	try	they	my
pay	sky	cry	day

Proofreading

Each sentence has two mistakes. Use the proofreading marks to fix each mistake. Write the misspelled List Words correctly on the lines.

Proofreading Marks
◯ spelling mistake
≡ capital letter

1. Rosa and john want to (tri) a new game.
— try

2. at the store, (thay) picked one to play.
— they

3. aunt Peggy gave them the money to (pey) for it.
— pay

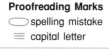

Spelling Superstar

Writing

Suppose one of these visitors knocked on your door. Write some sentences that tell what you would say.

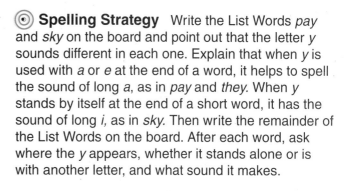

Spelling Strategy Write the List Words *pay* and *sky* on the board and point out that the letter *y* sounds different in each one. Explain that when *y* is used with *a* or *e* at the end of a word, it helps to spell the sound of long *a*, as in *pay* and *they*. When *y* stands by itself at the end of a short word, it has the sound of long *i,* as in *sky.* Then write the remainder of the List Words on the board. After each word, ask where the *y* appears, whether it stands alone or is with another letter, and what sound it makes.

Spelling Superstar   *Page 120*

Offer assistance as needed as students complete the **Writing** activity. Suggest that students fold their papers in half, so that their sentences are on the inside, and then draw a door on the cover. Students can trade papers with a partner and open the "door" to read the message.

✍ Writer's Corner

Students might enjoy hearing the knock-knock jokes in a book such as *Cricket's Jokes, Riddles and Other Stuff,* compiled by Marcia Leonard. Encourage students to jot down a favorite joke from the book, rehearse it with a partner, and perform it for the class.

Final Test

1. Please **try** to be on time.
2. Have you seen **my** toothbrush?
3. I will use pennies to **pay** for the book.
4. What a miserable, rainy **day** this is!
5. Do **they** still live in California?
6. The bird will fly **away** if you get close.
7. Look at the jet in the **sky.**
8. I hurt my toe, but I didn't **cry.**

Remind students to check their Final Tests against the List Words and to write any misspelled words in their Spelling Notebook.

★★ All-Star Words

July   dry   gray   maybe

With a partner, students can try to guess and write each All-Star Word as you finger-write it in the air. Afterward, write the All-Star Words on the board, pronouncing each one and discussing its meaning. Encourage students to write the words that they didn't guess correctly.

Lesson 30

Objective
To spell words in which *y* stands for the long *e* sound or part of the long *a* sound

Correlated Phonics Lessons
MCP Phonics, Level A, Lessons 113–114
Silver Burdett Ginn *World of Reading,* 1/5,
   pp. 232–233

Get Ready   *Page 121*
Read the directions aloud. Then read the poem with the class. Ask volunteers to repeat the lines they liked the best.

Get Set
Guide students as they look back at the words in dark print. Call on volunteers to say each word and name the vowel sound that *y* spells. Then go over the examples shown with the class.

Pretest
1. What a *funny* joke you told!
2. We were *happy* about winning the game.
3. How old is your *baby* brother?
4. Can my friends *stay* for lunch?
5. Jamie has *many* cats.
6. Our *puppy* is brown and white.
7. Carla put a saddle on the *pony.*
8. Today is *sunny,* so we are going swimming.

Go!   *Pages 122–124*
Read the List Words aloud with students. You may also want to read the directions aloud at the beginning of each exercise (**Sounds, Letters, and Words; ABC Order; Vocabulary; Story Puzzle**) and work through the first item with the class. As students complete the exercises, remind them to look back at their List Words or in their dictionaries if they need help.

 See **Words in Context,** page 14

88

---

y as a Vowel

Get Ready

Read the poem.

A **baby** dog is called a **puppy,**
and a kitten is a baby cat.
A baby fish is like a guppy.
There's nothing wrong with that!

No matter if it's small or big,
will a piglet **stay** a baby pig?
Even though it's cute and **funny,**
will a baby rabbit stay a bunny?

Get Set

Read the poem again. Say each word in dark print. Listen for the vowel sound the **y** spells.

> Sometimes the letter **y** has the long **e** sound, as in **baby, puppy,** and **funny.**
>
> The letter **y** helps to spell the long **a** sound in **spray.** What vowel sound does **y** help to spell in **stay?**

121

Go!

Sounds, Letters, and Words
Print each List Word under its heading.

LIST WORDS

1. baby
2. pony
3. funny
4. happy
5. stay
6. many
7. puppy
8. sunny

y spells /ē/

1. baby
2. pony
3. funny
4. happy
5. many
6. puppy
7. sunny

y helps to spell /ā/

8. stay

122   Lesson 30 ▪ y as a Vowel

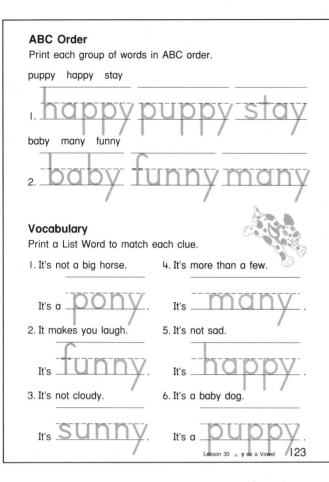

ABC Order
Print each group of words in ABC order.

puppy   happy   stay

1. happy puppy stay

baby   many   funny

2. baby funny many

Vocabulary
Print a List Word to match each clue.

1. It's not a big horse.

It's a pony.

2. It makes you laugh.

It's funny.

3. It's not cloudy.

It's sunny.

4. It's more than a few.

It's many.

5. It's not sad.

It's happy.

6. It's a baby dog.

It's a puppy.

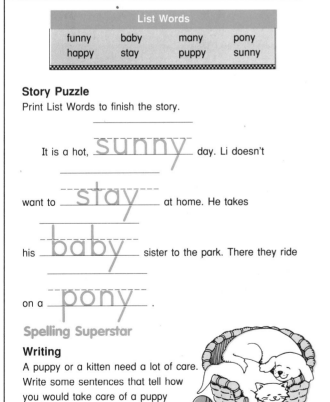

List Words			
funny	baby	many	pony
happy	stay	puppy	sunny

Story Puzzle
Print List Words to finish the story.

It is a hot, sunny day. Li doesn't

want to stay at home. He takes

his baby sister to the park. There they ride

on a pony.

Spelling Superstar

Writing
A puppy or a kitten need a lot of care.
Write some sentences that tell how
you would take care of a puppy
or kitten.

◎ Spelling Strategy   You may want to call out each List Word and have the class repeat it and spell it aloud. After each word, ask the class whether the letter *y* spells the long *e* sound or helps to spell the long *a* sound.

Spelling Superstar   *Page 124*
Offer assistance as needed as students complete the **Writing** activity. Students may want to share their writing by creating a poster that gives pet-care tips.

✍ Writer's Corner

> You may want to invite a veterinarian or an animal-shelter worker to visit your classroom and talk about pet care. Afterward, have the class write a thank-you note to send to the visitor.

Final Test
1. Otis was **happy** when he won the race.
2. Try not to wake the **baby.**
3. I am so excited that you can **stay!**
4. That clown was so **funny!**
5. How **many** children take the bus to school?
6. We got our **puppy** from an animal shelter.
7. I put the plant in a **sunny** spot.
8. The **pony** has a black mane and tail.

Remind students to check their Final Tests against the List Words and to write any misspelled words in their Spelling Notebook.

★★ All-Star Words

ladybug   family   hay   subway

Write the All-Star Words on the board and pronounce them for the class. Then hold up a picture from a book or a magazine that illustrates each word. With a partner, students can write the All-Star Word that goes with each picture.

Lesson 31 • Instant Replay

Objective
To review spelling words with *r, l,* and *s* blends; and *y* as a vowel

Time Out
Pages 125–128

Encourage students to look at the words in their Spelling Notebook. Ask which words in **Lessons 26–30** gave them the most trouble. Write the words on the board and offer assistance for spelling them correctly.

To give students extra help and practice in taking standardized tests, you may want to have them take the Review Test for this lesson on pages 92–93. After scoring the tests, return them to students so that they can record their misspelled words in their Spelling Notebook.

Before students begin each exercise for **Lessons 26–30,** you may want to go over the spelling rule, read the List Words and the directions aloud, and work through the first item with the class.

Take It Home Suggest that students ask family members to help them search through magazines and newspapers to collect List Words in **Lessons 26–30.** For a complete list of the words, have students take their *Spelling Workout* books home. Students can also use Take It Home Master 4 on pages 94–95 to help them do the activity. Invite students to share the words they found with the class.

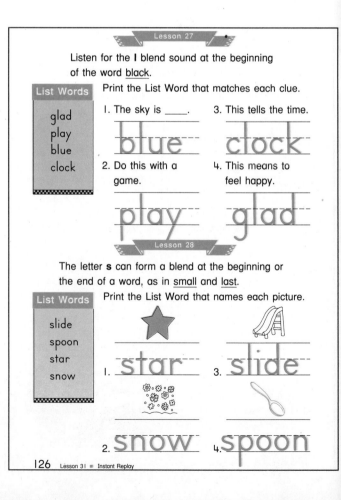

Time Out

Now it's time to review what you have learned about words with blends and **y** as a vowel.

Lesson 26

The letter **r** can form a blend when it follows another letter, as in <u>trap</u>.

List Words

from
drink
grow
brown

Unscramble each List Word. Print each word correctly.

1. nirdk   **drink**

2. rnobw   **brown**

3. wrog   **grow**

4. mrfo   **from**

125

Lesson 27

Listen for the **l** blend sound at the beginning of the word <u>black</u>.

List Words

glad
play
blue
clock

Print the List Word that matches each clue.

1. The sky is ____.   **blue**

2. Do this with a game.   **play**

3. This tells the time.   **clock**

4. This means to feel happy.   **glad**

Lesson 28

The letter **s** can form a blend at the beginning or the end of a word, as in <u>small</u> and <u>last</u>.

List Words

slide
spoon
star
snow

Print the List Word that names each picture.

1. **star**

2. **snow**

3. **slide**

4. **spoon**

126   Lesson 31 ▪ Instant Replay

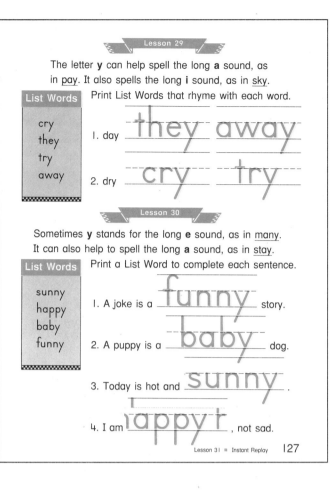

Lesson 29

The letter **y** can help spell the long **a** sound, as in <u>pay</u>. It also spells the long **i** sound, as in <u>sky</u>.

List Words

cry
they
try
away

Print List Words that rhyme with each word.

1. day   they   away

2. dry   cry   try

Lesson 30

Sometimes **y** stands for the long **e** sound, as in <u>many</u>. It can also help to spell the long **a** sound, as in <u>stay</u>.

List Words

sunny
happy
baby
funny

Print a List Word to complete each sentence.

1. A joke is a __funny__ story.

2. A puppy is a __baby__ dog.

3. Today is hot and __sunny__.

4. I am __happy__, not sad.

Lesson 31 ■ Instant Replay   127

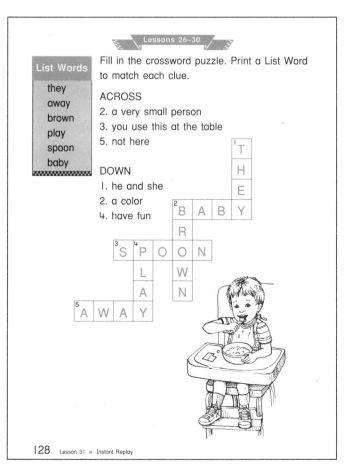

List Words

they
away
brown
play
spoon
baby

Fill in the crossword puzzle. Print a List Word to match each clue.

ACROSS
2. a very small person
3. you use this at the table
5. not here

DOWN
1. he and she
2. a color
4. have fun

(crossword puzzle)
1-down: T H E Y
2: B A B Y
3-across: S P O O N (4-down: P L A N)
2-down: B R O W N
5: A W A Y

128   Lesson 31 ■ Instant Replay

Final Replay Test   *Page 128*

1. Ask your friends if **they** can go to the movies.
2. The runner took a big **drink** of water.
3. My father and I have bright **blue** eyes.
4. Does the story have a **happy** ending?
5. Pine trees **grow** quickly.
6. I like to wear a hat on **sunny** days.
7. Does it ever **snow** where you live?
8. The baby will **cry** when he gets hungry.
9. The coach was **glad** her team had won.
10. Is a planet usually brighter than a **star?**
11. Everyone laughed at my **funny** story.
12. Please wear your **brown** shoes today.
13. The firefighters let us **slide** down the pole.
14. A **baby** deer is called a *fawn.*
15. Did you get a letter **from** your cousin?
16. That plan didn't work, so let's **try** another one.
17. Do we need four people to **play** this game?
18. Please move the plant **away** from that window.
19. Use this **spoon** when you eat your soup.
20. Oh, no! We forgot to set the alarm **clock!**

Remind students to check their Final Replay Tests against the List Words and to write any misspelled words in their Spelling Notebook.

Spelling Challenge

With a partner, students can circle and pronounce the consonant blends in the words in their Spelling Notebook. Also encourage students to look for *ey, ay,* and *y* and to tell the sound that *y* or vowel-*y* stands for in each word.

91

Instant Replay Test

Side A

Read each set of words. Fill in the circle next to the word that is spelled wrong.

1. (a) snoe   (c) small
   (b) trap   (d) spoon

2. (a) happy   (c) pony
   (b) clok   (d) stay

3. (a) black   (c) thay
   (b) green   (d) drink

4. (a) cry   (c) my
   (b) small   (d) awaye

5. (a) sky   (c) frum
   (b) drink   (d) broke

6. (a) babby   (c) spoon
   (b) my   (d) happy

7. (a) gladd   (c) cry
   (b) pay   (d) stay

Name _____

Instant Replay Test

Side B

Read each set of words. Fill in the circle
next to the word that is spelled wrong.

8.   ⓐ happy   ⓒ bloo

    ⓑ pay   ⓓ spoon

9.   ⓐ puppy   ⓒ suny

    ⓑ drink   ⓓ flag

10.   ⓐ slied   ⓒ clay

    ⓑ my   ⓓ fly

11.   ⓐ trap   ⓒ slow

    ⓑ play   ⓓ broun

12.   ⓐ drink   ⓒ pay

    ⓑ funney   ⓓ spoon

13.   ⓐ puppy   ⓒ starr

    ⓑ trap   ⓓ cry

14.   ⓐ trie   ⓒ fly

    ⓑ flag   ⓓ slow

15.   ⓐ groe   ⓒ clay

    ⓑ spoon   ⓓ drink

TAKE IT HOME

Your child has learned to spell many new words and would enjoy sharing them with you and your family. Read on for some ideas that will make reviewing the words in Lessons 26–30 as easy as A-B-C!

Word News

FINAL EDITION

What's in the news? Your child's spelling words! Help your child list words you find as you search through newspapers and magazines. Here's a clue—start with the ads!

from   drink   grow
brown   glad   play
blue   clock   slide
spoon   star   snow
cry   they   try   away
sunny   happy   baby
funny

Word Search

How many words can you and your child find in this puzzle?
Hint: Be sure to read across and down.

they	star	slide	spoon	glad	blue
grow	snow	play	brown	clock	cry

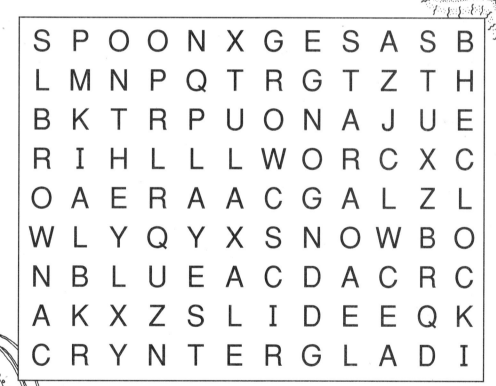

```
S P O O N X G E S A S B
L M N P Q T R G T Z T H
B K T R P U O N A J U E
R I H L L L W O R C X C
O A E R A A C G A L Z L
W L Y Q Y X S N O W B O
N B L U E A C D A C R C
A K X Z S L I D E E Q K
C R Y N T E R G L A D I
```

Lesson 32

Objective

To spell words with medial or final *th* digraphs and initial *wh* digraphs

Correlated Phonics Lessons

MCP Phonics, Level A, Lessons 117–118
MCP Discovery Phonics I, When It Snows/Little
  Bunny's Lunch
Silver Burdett Ginn *World of Reading,* 1/6, p. 157

Get Ready   *Page 129*

Read the directions aloud. Then read the sentences with the class. Ask students what they would like to do if they were at a summer camp for families.

Get Set

Guide students as they look back at the words in dark print. Call on volunteers to say each word and name the sound that *th* or *wh* spells. Then go over the examples shown with the class.

Pretest

1. **Where** do you usually buy groceries?
2. Anna knows **why** the bus is late.
3. We will have recess **when** the bell rings.
4. My **mother** is a doctor.
5. Mix the **white** and red paints to make pink.
6. My **father** tells the funniest jokes.
7. What a lot of trouble it is to give our dog a **bath!**
8. Can you walk to the library **with** me?

Go!   *Pages 130–132*

Read the List Words aloud with students, emphasizing the *th* or *wh* sound in each word. You may also want to read the directions aloud at the beginning of each exercise (**Sounds, Letters, and Words; Vocabulary; Puzzle; Proofreading**) and work through the first item with the class. As students complete the exercises, remind them to look back at their List Words or in their dictionaries if they need help.

 See **Student Dictation,** page 14

Get Ready

Read the sentences.

   Last summer **when** I went to camp, I didn't go alone. It was a summer camp for families. So my **mother** and **father** went **with** me!

   Mother learned to water ski. Father tried to weave a basket from straw, but it looked like a hat! I had lots of fun, especially watching them!

Get Set

Read the sentences again. Say each word in dark print. Listen for the **th** sounds and the **wh** sounds.

 When **w** and **h** come together, they make a new sound, as in the word **whale.** What sound do you hear at the beginning of the word **when?**

 When **t** and **h** come together, they make a new sound, as in the word **bath.** Listen for the **th** sound in the words **mother, father,** and **with.**

129

Go!

Sounds, Letters, and Words
Print the List Words with the sound **th.**

LIST WORDS

1. where
2. why
3. when
4. mother
5. white
6. father
7. bath
8. with

1. mother
2. father
3. bath   4. with

Print the List Words with the sound **wh.**

5. where
6. why
7. when
8. white

Vocabulary

Print a List Word to match each clue. Use the word shapes.

1. This asks at what time.

`w h e n`

2. This is your dad.

`f a t h e r`

3. This asks in what place.

`w h e r e`

4. This is your mom.

`m o t h e r`

5. This makes you clean.

`b a t h`

6. This asks for what reason.

`w h y`

Puzzle

Write the missing List Word in the correct box in the puzzle.

ACROSS
2. ___ do you like camp?
4. I play ___ my cat.
5. ___ is my cap?
6. He is my ___ .

DOWN
1. She is my ___ .
2. ___ will dinner be ready?
3. I have ___ teeth.

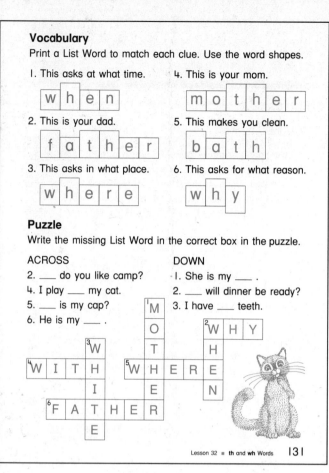

List Words			
where	when	white	bath
why	mother	father	with

Proofreading

Each sentence has two mistakes. Use the proofreading marks to fix each mistake. Print the misspelled List Words correctly on the lines.

Proofreading Marks
◯ spelling mistake
≡ capital letter

1. liz gave our dog Snowball a (bathe.)

2. she dried his fur (weth) a towel.

3. Now snowball is (wite) as snow.

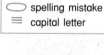

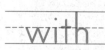

Spelling Superstar

Writing

If you went to a summer camp, what would you like to do? Write some sentences that tell what you would do to have fun.

◉ **Spelling Strategy**   Remind students that when some letters (*t* and *h*, *w* and *h*) come together, they make a new sound. Then say each List Word aloud and write it on the board. Call on a volunteer to come to the front of the class and point to the two letters that make a new sound. Underline the *th* or *wh* and call students' attention to its position in the word. Help students think of other words that have *th* or *wh* in the same position (i.e., *while, what, brother, other, teeth, path*).

Spelling Superstar   *Page 132*

Offer assistance as needed as students complete the **Writing** activity. Students may want to share their writing by using their sentences to create a postcard from "camp" to "mail" to a partner.

✍ Writer's Corner

Students might enjoy listening to the travelogue *Three Days on a River in a Red Canoe* by Vera B. Williams. After reading, invite students to pretend that they were on the trip described in the book and to write a few sentences about their experiences.

Final Test

1. Emily told me **why** she liked that book.
2. I wanted to play **with** my friend.
3. Do you know **where** I should put my coat?
4. My **father** likes to ride a bike.
5. I'll be ready **when** you get here.
6. My **mother** likes to jog, too.
7. What a beautiful vase of **white** flowers that is!
8. Do you like to take a shower or a **bath** at night?

Remind students to check their Final Tests against the List Words and to write any misspelled words in their Spelling Notebook.

★★ All-Star Words

tooth   feather   wheel   whisper

Write the All-Star Words on the board and pronounce them for the class. Then read the questions below. Encourage students to work with a partner to write the All-Star Word that answers each question.

1. What is round? (wheel)
2. What can tickle? (feather)
3. What is soft and quiet? (whisper)
4. What helps you chew? (tooth)

Lesson 33

Objective
To spell words with initial or final *sh* or *ch*

Correlated Phonics Lessons
MCP Phonics, Level A, Lessons 119–120
MCP Discovery Phonics I, Little Bunny's Lunch
Silver Burdett Ginn *World of Reading*, 1/6, p. 116; p. 157

Get Ready   *Page 133*
Read the directions aloud. Then read the sentences with the class. Ask students why they would or wouldn't like to eat the lunch that Julia Child is preparing.

Get Set
Guide students as they look back at the words in dark print. Call on volunteers to say each word and name the sound that *sh* or *ch* spells. You may also want to point out that Julia Child's last name begins with the *ch* sound. Then go over the examples shown with the class.

Pretest
1. We had to *chop* wood for the fire.
2. The *child* is in Mrs. Conti's kindergarten class.
3. What a great *lunch* we had today!
4. *She* is my best friend.
5. Who broke the *dish?*
6. Matthew will *show* you where to sit.
7. I bought this puzzle at the game *shop.*
8. When I kicked the ball, my *shoe* came off!

Go!   *Pages 134–136*
Read the List Words aloud with students, asking whether *sh* or *ch* appears at the beginning or end of the word. You may also want to read the directions aloud at the beginning of each exercise (**Sounds, Letters, and Words; Rhyming; Scrambled Letters; Puzzle**) and work through the first item with the class. As students complete the exercises, remind them to look back at their List Words or in their dictionaries if they need help.

 See **Charades/Pantomime**, page 15

---

sh and ch Words
LESSON **33**

Get Ready
Read the sentences.

The chef will **show** how to make **lunch.** **She** will **chop** the vegetables very carefully. She will cook them so that they taste delicious. Then she will put them in a **dish** and make them look beautiful. Her name is Julia Child.

Get Set
Read the sentences again. Say each word in dark print. Listen for the **sh** sounds and the **ch** sounds.

 When **s** and **h** come together they make a new sound, as in the word **shell.** Listen for the **sh** sound in the words **show** and **she.** What sound do you hear at the end of the word **dish?**

 When **c** and **h** come together, they make a new sound, as in the word **chair.** Listen for the **ch** sound in the words **chop** and **lunch.**

133

Go!
Sounds, Letters, and Words
Print the missing letters for each word. Trace the letters to spell List Words.

1. dish   5. chop
2. lunch   6. shoe
3. she   7. child
4. show   8. shop

LIST WORDS
1. chop
2. child
3. lunch
4. she
5. dish
6. show
7. shop
8. shoe

134 Lesson 33 ■ **sh** and **ch** Words

Rhyming

Print the List Word that rhymes with each word given.

1. wish   4. crunch

dish   lunch

2. he   5. glue

she   shoe

3. blow   6. wild

show   child

Scrambled Letters

Unscramble each List Word. Print the correct word on the line. The word shapes will help you.

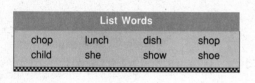

1. hisd   d i s h   4. chunl   l u n c h

2. esh   s h e   5. wsho   s h o w

3. hsop   s h o p   6. opch   c h o p

Lesson 33 ■ **sh** and **ch** Words   135

List Words			
chop	lunch	dish	shop
child	she	show	shoe

Puzzle

Fill in the crossword puzzle. Print a List Word to match each clue.

ACROSS
2. a young boy or girl
4. to cut up
5. it goes on your foot

DOWN
1. a place to buy things
3. a meal at noon

Spelling Superstar

Writing

What is your favorite dinner? Write some sentences that tell what you eat and how it is served.

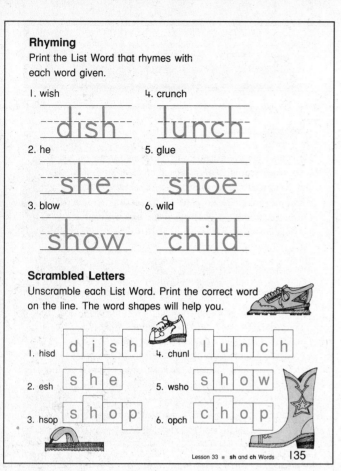

◉ **Spelling Strategy**   Explain to students that a digraph is a pair of letters that combine to make a new sound, and help them understand that they have already learned the digraphs *th, wh, sh,* and *ch.* Then read the List Words aloud with the class. After each, ask which digraph appears in the word and whether it appears at the beginning or at the end.

Spelling Superstar   *Page 136*

Offer assistance as needed as students complete the **Writing** activity. Students may want to share their writing by reading their sentences aloud as if they were famous television chefs.

✍ Writer's Corner

> Students might enjoy creating a menu for an imaginary restaurant. To stimulate ideas, you might want to display a variety of menus from restaurants in your area.

Final Test

1. Mother said *she* would take us swimming.
2. Lia will *chop* the carrots for the salad.
3. The police officer helped the *child* who fell.
4. I put the *shoe* on the wrong foot.
5. We will have sandwiches for *lunch* today.
6. Can you *show* me how to make a paper airplane?
7. Be careful or you'll break that *dish!*
8. Did you buy that present at the gift *shop?*

Remind students to check their Final Tests against the List Words and to write any misspelled words in their Spelling Notebook.

★★ All-Star Words

push   should   branch   chipmunk

After you write the All-Star Words on the board, pronounce them for the class and discuss their meanings. Then draw a word-shape box for each word. With a partner, students can write the All-Star Word that matches each box.

99

Lesson 34

Objective

To spell simple verbs with *ed* endings

Correlated Phonics Lessons

MCP Phonics, Level A, Lessons 115–116
Silver Burdett Ginn *World of Reading*, 1/6, p. 290

Get Ready   **Page 137**

Read the directions aloud. Then read the sentences with the class. Encourage students to tell something that they know about dinosaurs.

Get Set

Guide students as they look back at the words in dark print. Ask volunteers to say each word and name its ending. Then go over the examples shown with the class.

Pretest

1. We **asked** the zookeeper many questions.
2. Gilberto **looked** everywhere for the lost book.
3. I **needed** new sneakers for gym.
4. Who **fixed** her broken toy?
5. The parade **passed** by our house.
6. Were these hamburgers **cooked** on a grill?
7. Lionel **wanted** to help paint the fence.
8. Maggie **pulled** on the door handle.

Go!   **Pages 138–140**

Read the List Words aloud with students, emphasizing the *ed* ending in each word. You may also want to read the directions aloud at the beginning of each exercise (**Sounds, Letters, and Words; ABC Order; Vocabulary; Proofreading**) and work through the first item with the class. As students complete the exercises, remind them to look back at their List Words or in their dictionaries if they need help.

Before students begin the **Sounds, Letters, and Words** exercise, explain that all the List Words tell what has already happened. To reinforce this concept and to help students understand present and past tense, use the List Words and their present tense forms to complete the sentences *Today I _____* and *Yesterday I _____.*

 See **Comparing/Contrasting**, page 15

Get Ready

Read the sentences.

Dinosaurs lived millions of years ago. Some of these creatures **looked** like giant lizards. The biggest was Tyrannosaurus Rex. Rex was bigger than a house! He **needed** a lot of space to roam around. Rex liked plants, but he also **wanted** to eat meat. The other animals usually stayed out of his way!

Get Set

Read the sentences again. Look at the words in dark print. To make an action word tell what has already happened, you can add the ending **ed**.

 The word **cooked** tells about something that already happened. It ends with the sound for **ed**. Listen for the sounds at the end of the words **looked**, **needed**, and **wanted**. Do those words tell what has already happened?

137

Go!

Sounds, Letters, and Words

Add the letters **ed** to each word. Trace the letters to spell List Words.

LIST WORDS

1. asked
2. looked
3. needed
4. fixed
5. passed
6. cooked
7. wanted
8. pulled

1. needed
2. looked
3. cooked
4. asked
5. wanted
6. passed
7. fixed   8. pulled

138   Lesson 34 ■ Adding *ed* to Action Words

ABC Order

Print each group of List Words in ABC order.

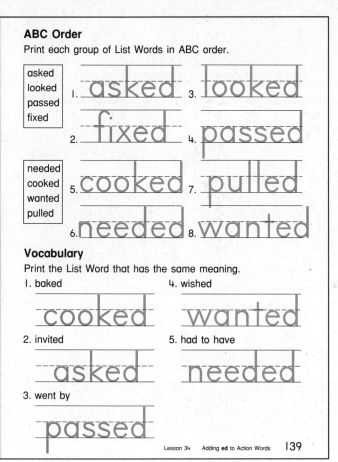

asked
looked
passed
fixed

1. asked
2. fixed
3. looked
4. passed

needed
cooked
wanted
pulled

5. cooked
6. needed
7. pulled
8. wanted

Vocabulary

Print the List Word that has the same meaning.

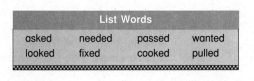

1. baked   cooked

2. invited   asked

3. went by   passed

4. wished   wanted

5. had to have   needed

List Words

asked	needed	passed	wanted
looked	fixed	cooked	pulled

Proofreading

Each sentence has two mistakes. Use the proofreading marks to fix each mistake. Print the misspelled List Words correctly on the lines.

Proofreading Marks

⬭ spelling mistake
⊙ add period

1. Tom (pulld) his wagon home⊙

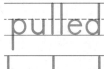 pulled

2. Dad (lookt) at Tom's wagon⊙

 looked

3. Then Dad (fixt) the flat tire⊙

 fixed

Spelling Superstar

Writing

Tyrannosaurus Rex was very big. What other big animals can you think of? Write a description of one of them.

Write two columns on the board, the first labeled *Present* and the second *Past*. Then write the present tense form of each List Word in the first column. Tell students that these words represent the present tense, or what happens *now*. Ask students what they should do to each word to tell what has *already happened* (add *ed*). Call on volunteers to write the past tense form of the words in the second column.

Spelling Superstar   *Page 140*

Offer assistance as needed as students complete the **Writing** activity. Students may want to share their writing by making drawings or clay models of the animals they described and displaying them with their descriptions.

✍ Writer's Corner

Students might enjoy listening to a book such as *Fossils Tell of Long Ago* by Aliki. Afterward, students can write the most interesting fact they learned and share it with a classmate.

Final Test

1. Tina **asked** if she could sit up front.
2. We **pulled** the sled up the hill.
3. Can the toaster be **fixed?**
4. Has the bus already **passed** by this stop?
5. The puppy **needed** a good home.
6. What a great meal Mrs. Wang **cooked** for us!
7. My sister **wanted** to go camping with her friends.
8. I **looked** for Lucas in the cafeteria.

Remind students to check their Final Tests against the List Words and to write any misspelled words in their Spelling Notebook.

★★ All-Star Words

crossed   played   picked   turned

Write the All-Star Words on the board and pronounce them for the class. Then write the sentences below on the board. Invite students to work with a partner to copy each sentence and complete it with the correct All-Star Word.

1. The children __(picked)__ flowers.
2. He __(played)__ in the park all day.
3. We __(crossed)__ the street.
4. Dad __(turned)__ on the light.

Lesson 35

Objective
To spell simple verbs that have *ing* endings

Correlated Phonics Lessons
MCP Phonics, Level A, Lessons 115–116
Silver Burdett Ginn *World of Reading*, 1/6, p. 310

Get Ready   **Page 141**
Read the directions aloud. Then read the poem with the class. Invite students to tell you what the picture shows.

Get Set
Guide students as they look back at the words in dark print. Call on volunteers to say each word and name the ending. Then go over the examples shown with the class.

Pretest
1. Is he *doing* all of the dishes?
2. Sherelle and Joe are *singing* in the talent show.
3. You are *being* very helpful today.
4. The wind is *blowing* leaves around the yard.
5. Kate is *rowing* the boat on the lake.
6. We are *having* so much fun playing this game!
7. Are we *going* to leave soon?
8. The boys are *sleeping* in a big tent.

Go!   **Pages 142–144**
Read the List Words aloud with students, emphasizing the *ing* ending in each word. You may also want to read the directions aloud at the beginning of each exercise (**Sounds, Letters, and Words; Vocabulary; ABC Order; Missing Words**) and work through the first item with the class. As students complete the exercises, remind them to look back at their List Words or in their dictionaries if they need help.

 See **Change or No Change,** page 15

102

Get Ready
Read the poem.

A breeze is **blowing.**
The stream is flowing.
There's no school today,
    and we're **going rowing.**
Having fun all day long,
    we'll be **singing** a song.
So why don't you come along?

Get Set
Read the poem again. Look at the words in dark print. To make an action word tell what is going on now, you can add the ending *ing.*

 The word **rowing** tells about something that is going on now. It ends with the sound for **ing.** Listen for the sounds at the end of the words **blowing, going, having,** and **singing.** Do those words tell what is going on now?

141

Go!
Sounds, Letters, and Words
Print the missing ending for each word. Trace the letters to spell List Words.

LIST WORDS
1. doing
2. singing
3. being
4. blowing
5. rowing
6. having
7. going
8. sleeping

1. sleeping
2. blowing
3. singing
4. rowing
5. having
6. doing
7. being
8. going

142   Lesson 35 ▪ Adding ing to Action Words

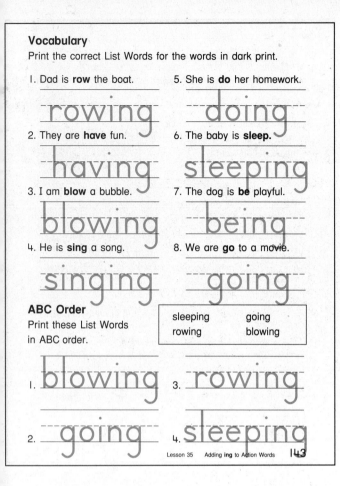

Vocabulary

Print the correct List Words for the words in dark print.

1. Dad is **row** the boat.

rowing

2. They are **have** fun.

having

3. I am **blow** a bubble.

blowing

4. He is **sing** a song.

singing

5. She is **do** her homework.

doing

6. The baby is **sleep.**

sleeping

7. The dog is **be** playful.

being

8. We are **go** to a movie.

going

ABC Order

Print these List Words in ABC order.

sleeping	going
rowing	blowing

1. blowing   3. rowing

2. going   4. sleeping

Lesson 35 ■ Adding **ing** to Action Words   143

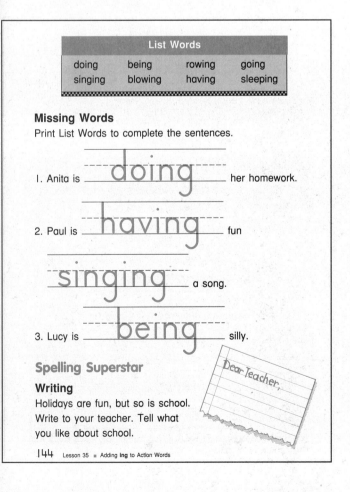

List Words			
doing	being	rowing	going
singing	blowing	having	sleeping

Missing Words

Print List Words to complete the sentences.

1. Anita is ___doing___ her homework.

2. Paul is ___having___ fun

___singing___ a song.

3. Lucy is ___being___ silly.

Spelling Superstar

Writing

Holidays are fun, but so is school. Write to your teacher. Tell what you like about school.

Dear Teacher,

144   Lesson 35 ■ Adding **ing** to Action Words

◎ **Spelling Strategy**   Write this sentence on the board: *I was row_____ the boat.* Read the sentence aloud (without the *ing*), and ask the class if it sounds right and makes sense. Then ask students what must be done to fix the sentence (add *ing* to *row*). Call on a volunteer to come to the board and fill in the missing ending, then read the corrected sentence aloud with the class. Repeat this procedure with other List Words. Remind students that they must drop the final *e* when adding *ing* to *have*.

Spelling Superstar   *Page 144*

Offer assistance as needed as students complete the **Writing** activity. Students can share their writing by putting their papers in a box on your desk, as if they are "mailing" them to you.

✍ **Writer's Corner**

> You may want to bring in some holiday greeting cards and share them with the class. Invite students to create a greeting card for an upcoming holiday and to give it to a special person on that day.

Final Test

1. The dog is *sleeping* in front of the fireplace.
2. Sally is *singing* a silly song.
3. Are you *having* trouble opening that jar?
4. *Blowing* up balloons can be tiring!
5. We took turns *rowing* the boat.
6. Do you think it is *going* to rain this morning?
7. Some people on the bus are *being* noisy.
8. Thomas is *doing* his chores.

Remind students to check their Final Tests against the List Words and to write any misspelled words in their Spelling Notebook.

★★ **All-Star Words**

watching   carrying   hiding   ringing

Write the roots of the All-Star Words on the board. Encourage students to work with a partner to add *ing* to each root, reminding them to drop the *e* in *hide* before adding the ending. Afterward, pronounce each All-Star Word and discuss its meaning with the class.

Lesson 36 • Instant Replay

Objective

To review spelling words with *th, wh, sh,* and *ch;* and the endings *ed* and *ing*

Time Out   *Pages 145–148*

Encourage students to look at the words in their Spelling Notebook. Ask which words in **Lessons 32–35** gave them the most trouble. Write the words on the board and offer assistance for spelling them correctly.

To give students extra help and practice in taking standardized tests, you may want to have them take the Review Test for this lesson on pages 106–107. After scoring the tests, return them to students so that they can record their misspelled words in their Spelling Notebook.

Before students begin each exercise for **Lessons 32–35,** you may want to go over the spelling rule, read the List Words and the directions aloud, and work through the first item with the class.

🏠 **Take It Home** Invite students to collect List Words in **Lessons 32–35** as they are riding in a car or a bus or taking a walk. Suggest that they look for the words on road signs, store signs, license plates, bumper stickers, and billboards. For a complete list of the words, have them take their *Spelling Workout* books home. Students can also use Take It Home Master 5 on pages 108–109 to help them do the activity. In class, encourage students to discuss their experiences finding words.

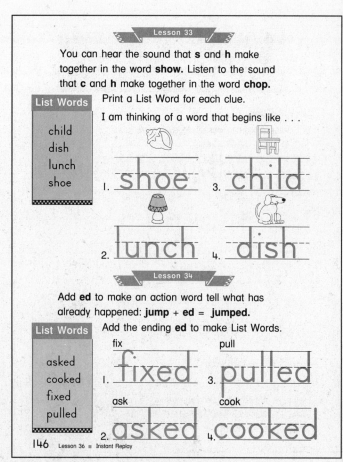

Name _____

Instant Replay • Lessons 32–35

Time Out

Take another look at the sounds **th** and **wh**, **sh** and **ch**, and adding **ed** or **ing** to action words.

Lesson 32

When **t** and **h** come together, they make a new sound, as in the word <u>father</u>. When **w** and **h** come together, they make a new sound, as in the word <u>why</u>.

List Words

mother
when
bath
white

Finish the story. Print a List Word in each blank. You may have to use a capital letter.

When it is time for bed, I first take a **bath**. Then I brush my **white** teeth. Then I kiss my **mother** good night.

145

Lesson 33

You can hear the sound that **s** and **h** make together in the word **show.** Listen to the sound that **c** and **h** make together in the word **chop.**

List Words

child
dish
lunch
shoe

Print a List Word for each clue.
I am thinking of a word that begins like . . .

1. **shoe**   3. **child**
2. **lunch**   4. **dish**

Lesson 34

Add **ed** to make an action word tell what has already happened: **jump + ed = jumped.**

List Words

asked
cooked
fixed
pulled

Add the ending **ed** to make List Words.

fix
1. **fixed**

pull
3. **pulled**

ask
2. **asked**

cook
4. **cooked**

146   Lesson 36 ■ Instant Replay

104

To tell about what is going on now, add **ing** to an action word: **go** + **ing** = **going.**

List Words

rowing
sleeping
singing
blowing

Print a List Word to tell what is going on in each picture.

1. _____

2. _____

3. _____

4. _____

Lesson 36   Instant Replay   147

Final Replay Test   *Page 148*

1. My cat is *white* and yellow.
2. Each *child* drew an interesting picture.
3. Uncle Ken *cooked* a delicious spaghetti dinner.
4. The baby is *sleeping* in the stroller.
5. Did your *mother* teach you how to swim?
6. Please fill the dog's *dish* with water.
7. Grandma *fixed* my broken bicycle.
8. The wind is *blowing* so hard today!
9. *When* you finish your picture, we'll hang it up.
10. Would you like a salad for *lunch?*
11. We *asked* the guard when the museum opened.
12. Look at how quickly they are *rowing* that boat!
13. Roberto gave his rabbit a *bath* in the sink.
14. Did you find your other soccer *shoe?*
15. They *pulled* open the heavy gate.
16. My dad enjoys *singing* in the choir.

Remind students to check their Final Replay Tests against the List Words and to write any misspelled words in their Spelling Notebook.

Spelling Challenge

Encourage students to categorize the words in their Spelling Notebook according to their digraphs (*th, wh, sh, ch*) or endings (*ed, ing*). Students can draw a line under the digraphs and circle the endings.

Solve the crossword puzzle. Print a List Word to match each clue.

List Words

when
mother
dish
child
fixed
needed
rowing
singing

ACROSS
4. another name for <u>Mom</u>
5. making musical sounds
7. repaired
8. a young person

DOWN
1. asks at what time
2. making a boat go
3. something to put food on
6. had to have

105

Instant Replay Test

Side A

Read each set of words. Fill in the circle next to the word that is spelled wrong.

1. ⓐ she   ⓒ doing
   ⓑ wite   ⓓ asked

2. ⓐ being   ⓒ rouing
   ⓑ when   ⓓ lunch

3. ⓐ bath   ⓒ pulled
   ⓑ passed   ⓓ cild

4. ⓐ sleeping   ⓒ looked
   ⓑ singging   ⓓ needed

5. ⓐ shop   ⓒ she
   ⓑ with   ⓓ muther

6. ⓐ fixxed   ⓒ dish
   ⓑ blowing   ⓓ where

7. ⓐ cooked   ⓒ shooe
   ⓑ shop   ⓓ bath

Instant Replay Test

Side B

Read each set of words. Fill in the circle
next to the word that is spelled wrong.

8. (a) having   (c) going
    (b) wen   (d) father

9. (a) show   (c) bloeing
    (b) with   (d) why

10. (a) wanted   (c) askt
    (b) chop   (d) singing

11. (a) mother   (c) bath
    (b) white   (d) pulld

12. (a) fixed   (c) child
    (b) luntch   (d) shoe

13. (a) with   (c) chop
    (b) rowing   (d) cookked

14. (a) sleping   (c) show
    (b) father   (d) having

15. (a) dishe   (c) wanted
    (b) why   (d) bath

5

TAKE IT HOME

Your child has learned to spell many new words in Lessons 32–35 and would like to share them with you and your family. The activity ideas on these pages can make sharing those words fun for the whole family.

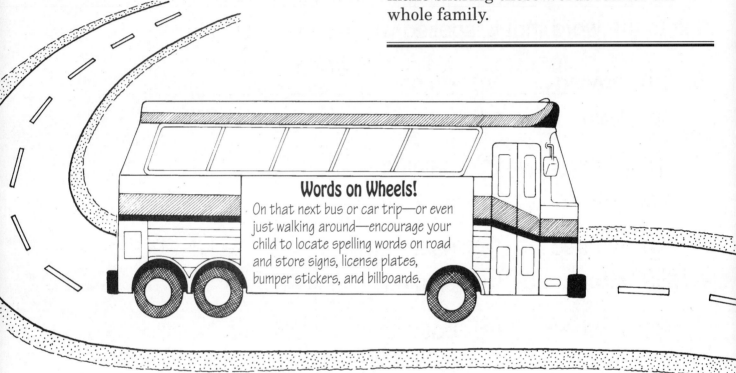

Words on Wheels!

On that next bus or car trip—or even just walking around—encourage your child to locate spelling words on road and store signs, license plates, bumper stickers, and billboards.

Crossword Puzzle

Here's a crossword puzzle for you and your child to solve. The words in the box will help you. Encourage your child to print the correct spelling word as you read aloud each clue.

rowing	child	white	singing
shoe	fixed	when	lunch

ACROSS

3. young boy or girl
4. making musical sounds
5. at what time?
6. repaired

DOWN

1. making a boat go
2. after breakfast, before dinner
4. a cover for your foot
5. color of milk

Writing and Proofreading Guide

Name each picture. Print each List Word that begins with the same sound as the picture name.

1. Choose something to write about.

2. Write your ideas. Don't worry about making mistakes.

3. Now proofread your work.
   Use these proofreading marks to check your work.

> **Proofreading Marks**
> ⬭ spelling mistake
> ≡ capital letter
> ⊙ add period

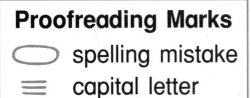

we have a new (pupy) at home⊙

4. Make your final copy.

   We have a new puppy at home.

5. Share your writing.

Spelling Workout Dictionary

Using Your Dictionary

The Spelling Workout Dictionary shows
you many things about your spelling
words.

The **entry word** listed in
ABC order is the word
you are looking up.

The **definition** tells us
what the word means.

fan   a thing used to move air to make it cool
[The air from the fan felt cool.] — fans

The **sample sentence**
show us how to use the
entry word.

Other **forms** of the word
are listed.

age   the time that a person or thing has existed from birth or beginning [Jan started school at the <u>age</u> of five.] —**ages**

and   I also [Tim <u>and</u> Jim like to run <u>and</u> play.] 2 added to [5 <u>and</u> 2 equals 7.]

around   I in a circle [The wheel turned <u>around</u>.] 2 in or to the opposite direction [We turned <u>around</u> and went back home.] 3 on all sides of [The flowers grew <u>around</u> the lake.] 4 about [Dad is <u>around</u> two inches taller than Mom.]

ask   I to use words to find out [I will <u>ask</u> her what her name is.] 2 to invite [Tom will <u>ask</u> Mike to his party.] —**asks, asked, asking**

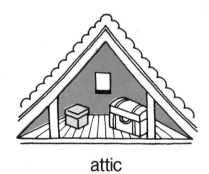

attic

attic   the room or space below the roof of a house [They found a box of old books in the <u>attic</u>.]

away   I to another place [The child ran <u>away</u> from the strange dog.] 2 in the proper place [Please put your toys <u>away</u>.] 3 not here [My sister is <u>away</u> today.]

ax   a tool for chopping or splitting wood [Dad chopped the firewood with an <u>ax</u>.] —**axes**

152

baby   a very young child [The <u>baby</u> cried for his bottle.] —**babies**

bag   paper, or other soft material made to carry things [I carry my lunch in a <u>bag</u>.] —**bags**

bake   to cook by dry heat [We will <u>bake</u> the cake in the oven for 30 minutes.] —**bakes, baked, baking**

balloon   **I** a large bag that floats when filled with a gas that is lighter than air [We saw the hot air <u>balloon</u> float across the sky.] **2** a rubber toy that can be blown up with air or gas [The clown gave us a <u>balloon</u> tied to a string.] —**balloons**

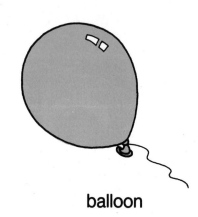

balloon

bark¹   the outside covering of the trunk and branches of a tree [The thick, black <u>bark</u> covered the logs.]

bark²   to make the sharp cry of a dog [The dog will <u>bark</u> at the stranger.] —**barks, barked, barking**

barn   a farm building for animals or machines [The cows slept in the <u>barn</u>.] —**barns**

barn

baseball   a game played with a ball and bat [The children played <u>baseball</u> in the summer.]

153

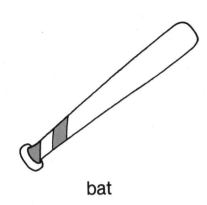

bat

bat[1] **1** a wooden club used in hitting the ball in baseball [Ryan hit the ball with a wooden bat.] **2** to hit with a bat [She will bat the ball over the fence.] —**bats, batted, batting**

bat[2] an animal that looks like a mouse but with wings of stretched skin [The bat flew out of the barn.] —**bats**

bath **1** the washing of something in water [We gave the dog a bath.] **2** the water used for bathing [The bath was too hot.] —**baths**

being **1** to be now [The baby is being quiet.] **2** a person [A human being is the smartest animal on earth.] —**beings**

best above all others in worth or ability [Laura is the best player on the team.]

big large [New York is a big city.] —**bigger, biggest**

bike

bike a toy to ride that has two wheels and two foot pedals [Ned rode his bike home.] —**bikes**

black the opposite color of white [The night sky was very black.]

blimp   an egg-shaped airship [The blimp floated over the football field.] —**blimps**

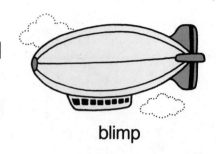

blimp

blow   I to move air out of the mouth [It is hard to blow up some balloons.] **2** to force air into to clear [I have to blow my nose.] **3** to make a sound by blowing [Did you hear the trumpet blow?] —**blows, blew, blown, blowing**

blue   I the color of the sky [The blue sky had fluffy, white clouds.] **2** sad [I felt blue when Dad left.] —**bluer, bluest**

boat   a small vessel for traveling on water [Lucy sailed the boat across the lake.] —**boats**

bold   ready to take risks or face danger; fearless [Columbus was a bold explorer.]

book   pages put together with a cover on the outside [It's fun to read a good book.] —**books**

both   two [Both babies are crying.]

box   a container made of cardboard or wood [Sam keeps his baseball cards in a box.]

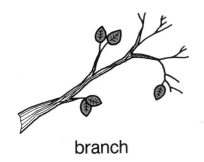

branch

branch part of a tree that grows from the trunk [A bird made a nest on the tree's top branch.] —**branches**

bridge something built over land or water to serve as a road across [The train crossed the bridge over the river.] —**bridges**

broke cracked into pieces [Abby broke the vase.] —**broken**

brown the color of chocolate or coffee [The tree's bark was brown.]

bus a large motor coach for carrying many passengers [Ed rode the bus to work.] —**buses**

but except [All the girls but Sara like to jump rope.]

butterfly

butterfly a brightly colored insect with wide wings [The caterpillar turned into a pretty butterfly.] —**butterflies**

buy to get by paying money [I will buy a new pencil with this coin.] —**buys, bought, buying**

156

Cc

came   moved from there to here [The cat came to eat.]

can[1]   is able to [Can a wish on a star come true?]

can[2]   a metal container [The tin can was full of peas.] —**cans**

car   anything that moves on wheels [Ron will park his car on the street.] —**cars**

carry   to take from one place to another [I carry books to school.] —**carries, carried, carrying**

cat   a pet with soft fur [My cat likes to play with yarn.] —**cats**

cat

cent   a coin worth a penny [What can I buy with one cent?] —**cents**

child   a young boy or girl [The child will play with that toy.] —**children**

chipmunk   a small squirrel of North America that lives in a hole in the ground [They saw a chipmunk at the park.] —**chipmunks**

chop   to cut with a sharp tool [Mom will chop the nuts with a knife.] —**chops, chopped, chopping**

157

clock

coat

coop

clay   stiff, sticky earth that gets hard when it is baked [We made <u>clay</u> pots in art class.]

clean   **1** without dirt [The car is shiny and <u>clean</u>.] **2** to make clean [Please <u>clean</u> your room.] —**cleaner, cleanest; cleans, cleaned, cleaning**

clock   a tool used to measure time [Su Lin looked at the <u>clock</u> to see if it was time to go.] —**clocks**

coat   an outer garment with sleeves that opens down the front [Kim's hat and gloves match her new <u>coat</u>.] —**coats**

cold   **1** chilly, not warm [A <u>cold</u> ice cream cone is good to eat on a hot day.] **2** an illness with sneezing, coughing, and a runny nose [Todd had a <u>cold</u> for a week.] —**colder, coldest, colds**

cook   to heat, boil, bake, or roast food [I like to <u>cook</u> hot dogs for lunch.] —**cooks, cooked, cooking**

coop   a cage or pen for small animals [The hens were kept in a chicken <u>coop</u>.] —**coops**

cross to go from one side to the other of [Amy and Joe <u>cross</u> the street.] —**crosses, crossed, crossing**

cry **1** to sob and shed tears when sad or in pain [Al tried not to <u>cry</u> when he got hurt.] **2** to say loudly [<u>Cry</u> for help if you need me.] —**cries, cried, crying**

cub a young bear or lion [The lion <u>cub</u> is very cute.] —**cubs**

cut to make an opening with a sharp tool [I <u>cut</u> the paper with scissors.] —**cuts, cut, cutting**

day **1** the time when it is light outside [Owls sleep during the <u>day</u>.] **2** the 24 hours from midnight to midnight [What <u>day</u> is your party?] —**days**

den **1** a cave or home for animals [The fox hid in his <u>den</u>.] **2** a small, cozy room [Ana likes to read in the <u>den</u>.] —**dens**

did has done [Max <u>did</u> his homework.]

dime a coin worth ten cents [I will trade this <u>dime</u> for two nickels.] —**dimes**

den

159

dog

dish   a plate or bowl used for food [I will put the meat on a clean <u>dish</u>.] —**dishes**

do   to work at [How long will it take you to <u>do</u> your homework?] —**does, did, done, doing**

doe   the female deer [The <u>doe</u> cared for her baby deer.] —**doe or does**

dog   a pet that can look like a fox or wolf [The little <u>dog</u> had a loud bark.] —**dogs**

down   to a lower place [The ball rolled <u>down</u> the hill.]

drink   to swallow a liquid [Don't <u>drink</u> the dirty water.] —**drinks, drank, drunk, drinking**

drop   to fall or let fall [Do not <u>drop</u> your coat on the floor.] —**drops, dropped, dropping**

drum   a musical instrument that is played by beating with sticks or the hands [Meg plays the <u>drum</u> in the school band.] —**drums**

dry   I not wet [The clothes are <u>dry</u> now.] **2** to make or become dry [Please <u>dry</u> the dishes.] —**drier, driest; dries, dried, drying**

duck[1]   a bird with a flat bill and webbed feet [The <u>duck</u> quacked at us.] —**ducks**

duck

duck²   to lower the head quickly [Duck if the ball comes this way.] —**ducks, ducked, ducking**

eat   to take in, chew, and swallow food [We will eat fruit for a snack.] —**eats, ate, eaten, eating**

egg   an oval shape that holds a baby bird until it is ready to be born [The hen laid one egg.] —**eggs**

end   **I** the last or farthest part [Gary went to sleep at the end of the day.] **2** to stop [When will the game end?] —**ends, ended, ending**

family   a group of people who are related [There are six children in Lana's family.] —**families**

fan   a thing used to move air to make it cool [The air from the fan felt cool.] —**fans**

fat   very plump [What a fat puppy!] —**fatter, fattest**

father   a man who has a child [The father took his son fishing.] —**fathers**

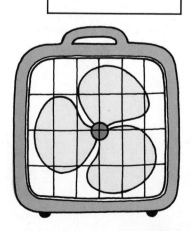

122

feather   one of the soft parts that cover birds [The parrot lost a green <u>feather</u>.] —**feathers**

feet   **1** parts of the body at the end of one's legs used to stand on [Lisa wore shoes on her <u>feet</u>.] **2** more than one set of twelve inches [A yardstick is three <u>feet</u> long.]

fish

fence   a wall of wood or wire put around a yard [Our yard has a white <u>fence</u>.] —**fences**

fill   to make something full [John will <u>fill</u> the pail with water.] —**fills, filled, filling**

firefly   a small beetle whose lower body glows [The light of the <u>firefly</u> blinks off and on at night.] —**fireflies**

fish   an animal with fins and gills that lives in water [<u>Fish</u> swim in the lake.]

five   the number after four [I have <u>five</u> fingers on each hand.]

flag

fix   to make something right [Dad tried to <u>fix</u> the broken bike.] —**fixes, fixed, fixing**

flag   a cloth with colors or pictures on it [We waved a red, white, and blue <u>flag</u>.] —**flags**

flashlight   an electric light that uses batteries and is small enough to carry [Sal used a <u>flashlight</u> to see into the cave.] —**flashlights**

fly¹   to move in the air with wings [I saw the bird <u>fly</u> away.] —**flies, flew, flown, flying**

fly²   a tiny insect [The <u>fly</u> came in when James went out.] —**flies**

fold   to bend one part of a thing over another part [I will <u>fold</u> the paper in half.] —**folds, folded, folding**

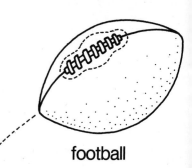

football

follow   to come or go after [The dog wanted to <u>follow</u> me.] —**follows, followed, following**

food   a thing we eat to live and grow [The <u>food</u> was cooked on the stove.] —**foods**

football   a game played with an oval ball [Jan will kick the <u>football</u> over the goal.]

found   got by looking [Pete <u>found</u> a dime.]

fox   a wild animal that has pointed ears and a bushy tail [The <u>fox</u> lives in a den.] —**foxes**

freeze   to harden into ice [The lakes <u>freeze</u> in winter.] —**freezes, froze, freezing**

frog

frog   a small pond animal that hops or makes a croaking sound [The tadpole grew into a <u>frog</u>.] —**frogs**

from   I starting at [The store is open <u>from</u> nine until five.] **2** out of [Take your coat <u>from</u> the closet.] **3** sent by [She got a gift <u>from</u> me.]

frown   to show that one does not like something [My parents <u>frown</u> when I am late.] —**frowns, frowned, frowning**

fun   a happy time [We had <u>fun</u> at the party.]

funny   makes one laugh [The <u>funny</u> clown had a red nose.] —**funnier, funniest**

game   a form of play [We like the <u>game</u> of hide-and-seek.] —**games**

gave   handed over [I <u>gave</u> the book to him.]

girl   a female child [That <u>girl</u> is my sister.] —**girls**

glad   happy [I am <u>glad</u> that you like me.] —**gladder, gladdest**

glass   a hard substance that breaks easily and lets light through [The window is made of <u>glass</u>.] —**glasses**

go   to move from one place to another [Becky will go home at six.] —**goes, went, gone, going**

got   came to own [Fred got a new bike.]

gray   I a color made by mixing black and white [The cat had gray fur. **2** to be dark or dull [The gray clouds will bring rain.]

great   very important [She is a great pianist.] —**greater, greatest**

green   the color of grass [Fran painted the room green.]

grin   to give a big smile [The clown made the children grin.] —**grins, grinned, grinning**

ground   land; earth [Mike planted a flower in the ground.]

grow   to get larger or older [The child will grow taller next year.] —**grows, grew, grown, growing**

---

hand   part of the body at the end of one's arm [I am holding a coin in my hand.] —**hands**

happy   glad [I am happy to see you!] —**happier, happiest**

126

hat

has   owns or holds [That camel <u>has</u> two humps.] —**have, had, having**

hat   a thing used to cover the head [Dan put a <u>hat</u> on his head to keep warm.] —**hats**

have   own or hold [I <u>have</u> red hair.] —**has, had, having**

hay   grass or clover that is cut and dried for use as food for animals [Horses eat <u>hay</u>.]

heat   hot air that can be felt [The <u>heat</u> of the fire made us warm.]

hide   to put or keep out of sight [<u>Hide</u> the present in the closet.] —**hides, hid, hiding**

him   the form of HE that is used as the object of a verb or preposition [The dog jumped on <u>him</u>.]

hit   to bump or knock [The car <u>hit</u> the tree.] —**hits, hit, hitting**

home   the place where one lives [Matt's <u>home</u> is on Front Street.] —**homes**

hook   curved metal that will catch or hold something [I hung my coat on a <u>hook</u>.] —**hooks**

hop   to move in short jumps [The frog will <u>hop</u> into the pond.] —**hops, hopped, hopping**

hopscotch   a game where children hop from one space to another [<u>Hopscotch</u> squares were on the sidewalk.]

hot   very warm [I burned my hand on the <u>hot</u> stove.] —**hotter, hottest**

house   a building where one lives [We will play at Molly's <u>house</u>.] —**houses**

how   in what way [<u>How</u> did you get home?]

hug   to hold close in a loving way [I will <u>hug</u> my teddy bear.] —**hugs, hugged, hugging**

hunt   to try to find [I had to <u>hunt</u> for my homework.] —**hunts, hunted, hunting**

---

ice   water frozen solid [Vicky skated on the <u>ice</u>.]

167

jar a wide glass container [The lid on the jam jar was open.] —**jars**

jet a fast airplane [The jet made a white trail in the sky.] —**jets**

job any work one has to do [My job is to take out the trash.] —**jobs**

jog to run slowly [Paul will jog in the park.] —**jogs, jogged, jogging**

joke a funny story [The joke made me laugh.] —**jokes**

July the seventh month of the year [We go to the beach in July.]

jump to leap [Laura had to jump to get the ball.] —**jumps, jumped, jumping**

just 1 only [I am just being silly.] 2 by a small amount [You just missed a phone call.]

kick to strike with the foot [Kick the ball.] — **kicks, kicked, kicking**

kite a toy that flies in the wind [Fly your kite on a windy day.] —**kites**

ladybug   a small spotted beetle [A ladybug can be red with black spots.] —**ladybugs**

lamp   a thing that gives light [The lamp lit our bedroom.] —**lamps**

last   after all others [Maria was the last one in line.]

late   happening or coming after the usual or expected time [Jody was late for school.] —**later, latest**

ladybug

leg   part of the body used for standing [Jeff's legs hurt from running.] —**legs**

like   to enjoy [June likes dogs.] —**likes, liked, liking**

lock   to fasten a door or safe. We lock our doors at night.] —**locks, locked, locking**

log   a section of a tree that has been cut [Dad put a log in the fire.] —**logs**

look   to see with one's eyes [Carlos will look at the nice sunset.] —**looks, looked, looking**

lot   very much [Grace felt a lot happier when she saw her lost pet.]

lunch

luck good or bad things that seem to happen by chance [It was good <u>luck</u> that I won.]

lunch a small meal eaten a few hours after breakfast [We like to eat <u>lunch</u> at noon.] —**lunches**

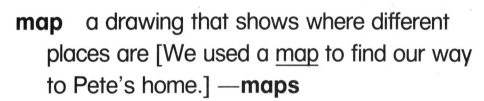

make to bring into being [Mom will <u>make</u> lunch for us.] —**makes, made, making**

man an adult male [The <u>man</u> you met is my father.] —**men**

many a large number of [She read <u>many</u> books about dogs.] —**more, most**

map a drawing that shows where different places are [We used a <u>map</u> to find our way to Pete's home.] —**maps**

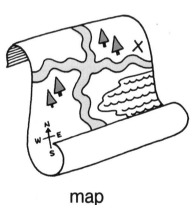

map

mask something worn over the face [Kathy wore a scary Halloween <u>mask</u>.] —**masks**

maybe perhaps [<u>Maybe</u> we can go to the park tomorrow.]

meal breakfast, lunch, or dinner [Lunch is Bob's favorite <u>meal</u>.] —**meals**

milk something white to drink that comes from cows [The cow's <u>milk</u> was sweet.]

mine   something that belongs to me [The pen you found is <u>mine</u>.]

mix   to stir or join together [Let's <u>mix</u> nuts into the cookie batter.] —**mixes, mixed, mixing**

mother   a woman who has a child [The <u>mother</u> loves her baby.] —**mothers**

mouse   a small animal found in houses and fields [The <u>mouse</u> ran from the cat.] —**mice**

mouse

mud   wet earth that is soft and sticky [The dog rolled in the <u>mud</u>.]

my   of me [<u>My</u> house is on First Street.]

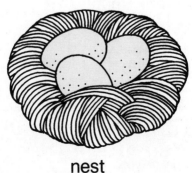

name   a word for a person, place, or thing [My friend's <u>name</u> is Mary Pate.] —**names**

neat   clean and tidy [Dale keeps his room <u>neat</u>.] —**neater, neatest**

neck   the part that joins the head to the body [She wore a scarf around her <u>neck</u>.] —**necks**

need   to want [I <u>need</u> a stamp to mail this letter.] —**needs, needed, needing**

nest

nest   a home made by a bird [The robin's eggs
were in the <u>nest</u>.] —**nests**

not   in no way [My mom was <u>not</u> happy to see the mud on my feet.]

off   not on [Take your hat <u>off</u> and put it on the hook.]

one   the number before two [You may eat only <u>one</u> piece of cheese at a time.]

ouch   a sound made to show sudden pain [When he fell, he cried, "<u>Ouch</u>!"]

our   the one that belongs to us [We will paint the trim on <u>our</u> house red.]

out   away from the inside [Cathy will take the dog <u>out</u> for a walk.]

owl   a bird with large eyes, large head, a short beak, and sharp claws [The <u>owl</u> hunts at night.] —**owls**

pass   I go by [We <u>pass</u> your house each day.] 2 to move [Please <u>pass</u> the bread to me.] —**passes, passed, passing**

paste   a mixture of flour and water that is used for sticking things together [Barbara used <u>paste</u> to put her photos in the book.]

172

pay to give money for something [Did you pay for the paper?] —**pays, paid, paying**

pen a tool used to write with ink [We write with a pen in fifth grade.] —**pens**

pen

penny a coin worth one cent [Cora put the shiny, new penny in her bank.] —**pennies**

pick to choose or select [The judge will pick the winner.] —**picks, picked, picking**

pig a farm animal raised for its meat [The pig had pink skin and a short tail.] —**pigs**

pill a tablet of medicine [Joan gave the sick dog a pill.] —**pills**

pig

pin a stiff, pointed wire used to hold things together [We put our name tags on with a pin.] —**pins**

pipe a long tube through which a liquid can flow [The water flowed through a pipe.] —**pipes**

place 1 a space or spot [This is a good place to rest.] 2 to put somewhere [Place the pencil on the desk.] —**places, placed, placing**

plane

plane   an aircraft [The <u>plane</u> flew above the clouds.] —**planes**

play   to have fun [It is fun to <u>play</u> baseball.] —**plays, played, playing**

pond   a small lake [The cows drank from the <u>pond</u>.] —**ponds**

pony   a type of small horse [We rode on a <u>pony</u> at the fair.] —**ponies**

pop   I a short, loud sound [We heard a <u>pop</u> when the balloon broke.] **2** sweet soda drink [I like to drink cherry <u>pop</u>.] —**pops**

pot   a round container used for cooking or holding things [Dad cooked the soup in a <u>pot</u>.] —**pots**

pull   to move something nearer [The boy must <u>pull</u> his sled up the hill.] —**pulls, pulled, pulling**

puppet   a small figure moved by strings or the hands [Alicia made the <u>puppet</u> dance.] —**puppets**

pup, puppy   a young dog [The little <u>puppy</u> barked and jumped.] —**puppies**

push to press against so as to move [I had to push my bike up the hill.] —**pushes, pushed, pushing**

queen a woman who rules a country [The queen wears a gold crown.] —**queens**

quick done with speed [We made a quick trip to the store.]

ran moved very fast [The dog ran after the ball.]

red the color of blood [I ate a red apple.] —**redder, reddest**

rest to keep still [The baby will rest in the crib.] —**rests, rested, resting**

ride to sit on and move [Beth will ride in the car.] —**rides, rode, ridden, riding**

ring¹ I to make the sound of a bell [The phone will ring.] 2 to cause a bell to sound [Ring the doorbell.] —**rings, rang, ringing**

ring² a thin band shaped like a circle and worn on a finger [Nina wore a silver ring.] —**rings**

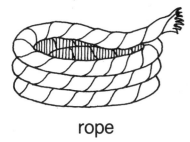

rope

road   a way for cars and trucks to go from place to place [The dirt <u>road</u> was bumpy.] —**roads**

rock   a large stone [I sat on the <u>rock</u>.] —**rocks**

rope   a thick cord [Keisha tied a <u>rope</u> to the tree.] —**ropes**

row¹   people or things in a line [Juan sits in the first <u>row</u>.] —**rows**

row²   to move a boat using oars [Debbie had to <u>row</u> the boat to shore.] —**rows, rowed, rowing**

rowboat

rowboat   a boat that uses oars to move [Don used oars to move the <u>rowboat</u> across the pond.] —**rowboats**

rug   a thing that covers floors [The <u>rug</u> kept the floor clean.] —**rugs**

run   to move with the legs very fast [Sara had to <u>run</u> to catch the bus.] —**runs, ran, run, running**

seal   a sea animal with four flippers [The <u>seal</u> swam underwater.] —**seals**

see   to look at [Did you <u>see</u> me in the window?] —**sees, saw, seen, seeing**

set   to put in a certain place or position [Beth <u>set</u> the book on the table.] —**sets, set, setting**

seven   the number after six [There are <u>seven</u> days in a week.]

she   a girl or woman being talked about [Liz said that <u>she</u> found a key.]

sheep   a farm animal that is covered with wool [A lamb is a baby <u>sheep</u>.]

shell   a hard covering [I found a snail's <u>shell</u> on the beach.] —**shells**

shirt   a thing to wear on top of the body [Dad wore a <u>shirt</u> and tie.] —**shirts**

shoe   a cover for the foot [My <u>shoe</u> is made of leather.] —**shoes**

shop   to go to the store to buy something [Jean must <u>shop</u> for a new coat.] —**shops, shopped, shopping**

Ss

sheep

shirt

shoe

177

should   a helping verb used to speak of something that one ought to do [We should always do our homework.]

show   to let a person see something [Will you show us your new dress?] —**shows, showed, shown, showing**

sing   to make music with the voice [She can sing very well.] —**sings, sang, sung, singing**

sit   to bend at the waist to rest on one's bottom [We must sit down all day at school.] —**sits, sat, sitting**

six   the number after five [There are six months in half a year.]

sky   the air above the earth [We could see clouds floating in the blue sky.] —**skies**

sled   a low platform on runners, used for riding over the snow [Paula zoomed down the hill on her sled.] —**sleds**

sleep   to close one's eyes and rest [Paulo can sleep only if it is dark.] —**sleeps, slept, sleeping**

slide a playground toy with a long, slanted board [Lynn likes to go down the <u>slide</u>.] —**slides**

slow not fast [The baby liked the <u>slow</u> ride in the wagon.] —**slower, slowest**

small little [The grapes were <u>small</u>.] —**smaller, smallest**

smile to show that one is happy [The gift made Maria <u>smile</u>.] —**smiles**

snail a soft, slow-moving animal that lives in a spiral shell [A <u>snail</u> can live on land or in the water.] —**snails**

snow soft, white flakes that fall from the sky in cold weather [Ken likes to ride a sled in the <u>snow</u>.]

soap a thing that makes suds to wash with [Lou cleaned her hands with <u>soap</u> and water.] —**soaps**

south direction toward the left when you face the sunset [Many birds fly <u>south</u> in the fall.]

speak to talk [They <u>speak</u> to each other on the phone.] —**speaks, spoke, speaking**

slide

snail

spoon a tool for eating or stirring [Fred ate soup with a <u>spoon</u>.] —**spoons**

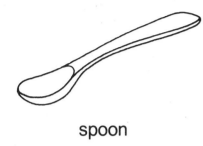

spoon

spot a small mark [Missy has a <u>spot</u> of mud on her sock.] —**spots**

stand to be or get on one's feet [<u>Stand</u> by your desk.] —**stands, stood, standing**

star **1** a small, bright light in the night sky [That bright <u>star</u> is very far away.] **2** a shape with five points [Miss Jones put a gold <u>star</u> on my paper.] —**stars**

star

stay to not move from one place [Ken had to <u>stay</u> in bed when he was sick.] —**stays, stayed, staying**

step to move the foot [Take one <u>step</u> backward.] —**steps**

stick a twig or branch [Linda used a small <u>stick</u> to draw in the sand.] —**sticks**

stop to quit moving [The bus will <u>stop</u> to let the man off.] —**stops, stopped, stopping**

subway an underground electric railway [Dad rides the <u>subway</u> to work.] —**subways**

summer a time of the year after spring [We like to swim in the <u>summer</u>.]

sun   a large body in the sky that gives us light and heat [The <u>sun</u> shines during the day.]

sunny   bright from the sun [It can get hot on <u>sunny</u> days.] —**sunnier, sunniest**

surf   the white foam of waves [It is fun to float on the <u>surf</u>.]

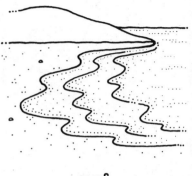

surf

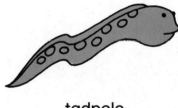

tadpole   a young frog [The <u>tadpole</u> has a tail.] —**tadpoles**

tag   a chasing game [Chad chased me when we played <u>tag</u>.]

take   to get [I will <u>take</u> a turn if you let me.] —**takes, took, taking**

tame   no longer wild [Andrea has a <u>tame</u> rabbit for a pet.]

teach   to show or help to learn how to do something [Mom is going to <u>teach</u> me how to play chess.] —**teaches, taught, teaching**

tadpole

ten   the number after nine [I have <u>ten</u> toes.]

thank   to say to someone you like the kindness they did for you [I will <u>thank</u> Grandma for the gift.] —**thanks, thanked, thanking**

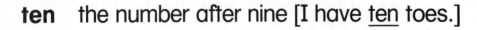

181

they   persons or animals being talked about [Chris and Joe said <u>they</u> missed the bus.]

this   a thing being talked about [<u>This</u> food tastes good.]

three   the number after two [A clover has <u>three</u> leaves.]

time   minutes, hours, days, and years [It took a long <u>time</u> to learn to tie my shoes.]

toad

toad   an animal like a frog that lives on land [A <u>toad</u> hopped out of the garden.] —**toads**

toe   one of the five parts at the end of the foot [Tess stepped on my big <u>toe</u>.] —**toes**

tooth   a bony, white part of the mouth used to bite and chew [Amy brushes each <u>tooth</u> carefully.] —**teeth**

top¹   the highest part [David went to the <u>top</u> of the hill.]

top

top²   a child's toy that spins [Carrie made the <u>top</u> spin.] —**tops**

train   a line of railroad cars [We took a <u>train</u> to see my aunt.] —**trains**

182

trap   a tool for catching animals [The mouse was in the <u>trap</u>.] —**traps**

tree   a large plant with branches and leaves [Wood comes from the trunk of a <u>tree</u>.] —**trees**

trunk   I the main part of a tree [The bark on the tree's <u>trunk</u> was smooth.] **2** an elephant's nose [The elephant picked up a nut with his <u>trunk</u>.] —**trunks**

try   to work on [Bill will <u>try</u> to pick up the heavy log.] —**tries, tried, trying**

tub   a thing that holds water for a bath [Ali washed the baby in the <u>tub</u>.] —**tubs**

turtle

turn   to move around a center point [The wheels of the car <u>turn</u>.] —**turns, turned, turning**

turtle   an animal with a hard shell, four legs, and a tail [A <u>turtle</u> can live on land or in water.] —**turtles**

us you and me [Dad took <u>us</u> to the park.]

van a closed truck [We took our bikes in the back of the <u>van</u>.] —**vans**

very a big amount [I am <u>very</u> hungry.]

vest a short garment without sleeves [Marcos wore a <u>vest</u> under his jacket.] —**vests**

vine any plant with a long, thin stem that grows along the ground or climbs walls or trees, by fastening itself to them [The ivy <u>vine</u> grew up the walls.] —**vines**

wait to stay in place or do nothing [<u>Wait</u> for the bell.] —**waits, waited, waiting**

wall the flat side of a room [We hung a painting on the <u>wall</u>.] —**walls**

want to wish for [Lin and Sherry <u>want</u> a new bike.] —**wants, wanted, wanting**

watch   to look at [We <u>watch</u> the parade.]
—**watches, watched, watching**

we   you and I [<u>We</u> want to eat lunch.]

weed   a plant that grows where it is not
wanted [David pulled the ugly <u>weed</u> out of
his garden.] —**weeds**

went   to be gone [We <u>went</u> to visit Carla.]

west   toward the point where the sun sets [We
saw the sun set in the <u>west</u>.]

west

wet   not dry [Water dripped from the <u>wet</u> rag.]
—**wetter, wettest**

wheel   a round disk or frame that turns [I bent
the front <u>wheel</u> on my bike.] —**wheels**

when   at what time? [<u>When</u> did you eat
lunch?]

where   at what place? [<u>Where</u> are my
glasses?]

whisper   to speak in a low, soft voice [<u>Whisper</u>
the secret to me.] —**whispers, whispered,
whispering**

white   the color of clean snow or milk [The
bride wore a <u>white</u> dress.] —**whiter, whitest**

146   185

why   for what reason? [Why did Bob go home?]

will   a word that shows something is yet to be done [Pam will leave soon.]

win   to get by work or skill [Brian wants to win the prize.] —**wins, won, winning**

with   **1** in the care of [I went to the show with my mom.] **2** into [Mix blue with yellow to get green.] **3** having [The girl with the red coat is my friend.]

Yy

yes   the opposite of NO [Yes, I will eat my dinner.]

you   the person or persons talked to [You are my best friend.]

Zz

zebra   a wild animal of Africa that has dark stripes on a white or tan body [We saw a zebra in the zoo.] —**zebras**

zip   to join with a zipper [Neil will zip his coat to keep warm.] —**zips, zipped, zipping**

zoo   a place to see wild animals [The tigers at the zoo are kept in cages.] —**zoos**

Level A Student Record Chart

Name _____

			Pretest	Final Test
Lesson 1	Beginning and Ending Sounds			
Lesson 2	Alphabet Review			
Lesson 3	Sounds and Letters **A–N**			
Lesson 4	Sounds and Letters **O–Z**			
Lesson 5	Matching Sounds and Letters			
Lesson 6	Beginning and Ending **s, t, b**			
Lesson 7	Beginning and Ending **h, m, p, k**			
Lesson 8	Beginning and Ending **j, f, g**			
Lesson 9	Beginning and Ending **l, d, n**			
Lesson 10	Beginning and Ending **w, c, r**			
Lesson 11	Beginning **v, y, z, qu**			
Lesson 12	Ending **x, k, p**			
Lesson 13	Instant Replay		■■■■■	
Lesson 14	Short **a** Sound			
Lesson 15	Short **i** Sound			
Lesson 16	Short **u** Sound			
Lesson 17	Short **o** Sound			
Lesson 18	Short **e** Sound			
Lesson 19	Instant Replay		■■■■■	
Lesson 20	Long **a** Sound			
Lesson 21	Long **i** Sound			
Lesson 22	Long **o** Sound			
Lesson 23	Long **e** Sound			
Lesson 24	**ou** Sound			
Lesson 25	Instant Replay		■■■■■	
Lesson 26	**r** Blends			
Lesson 27	**l** Blends			
Lesson 28	**s** Blends			
Lesson 29	**y** as a Vowel			
Lesson 30	**y** as a Vowel			
Lesson 31	Instant Replay		■■■■■	
Lesson 32	**th** and **wh** Words			
Lesson 33	**sh** and **ch** Words			
Lesson 34	Adding **ed** to Action Words			
Lesson 35	Adding **ing** to Action Words			
Lesson 36	Instant Replay		■■■■■	

Lesson	13	19	25	31	36
Standardized Instant Replay Test					

Instant Replay Test

ANSWER KEY

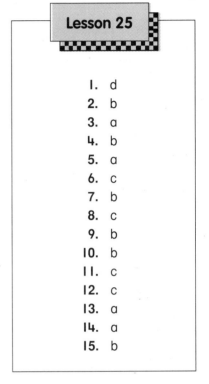

Lesson 13

1. a
2. d
3. c
4. d
5. a
6. b
7. b
8. b
9. a
10. d
11. d
12. a
13. c
14. d
15. b

Lesson 19

1. c
2. a
3. b
4. d
5. c
6. a
7. b
8. d
9. a
10. a
11. d
12. d
13. c
14. a
15. d

Lesson 25

1. d
2. b
3. a
4. b
5. a
6. c
7. b
8. c
9. b
10. b
11. c
12. c
13. a
14. a
15. b

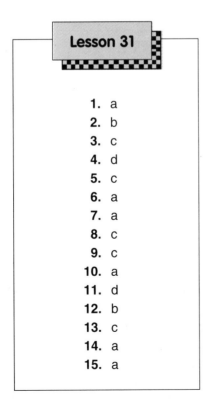

Lesson 31

1. a
2. b
3. c
4. d
5. c
6. a
7. a
8. c
9. c
10. a
11. d
12. b
13. c
14. a
15. a

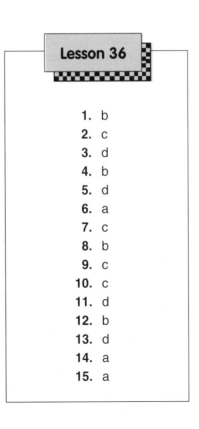

Lesson 36

1. b
2. c
3. d
4. b
5. d
6. a
7. c
8. b
9. c
10. c
11. d
12. b
13. d
14. a
15. a

List Words

Word	Lesson	Word	Lesson	Word	Lesson	Word	Lesson
and	14	five	21	mine	21	spot	28
around	24	fixed	34	mix	12	star	28
asked	34	flag	27	mother	32	stay	30
away	29	fly	27	mouse	24	stop	7
baby	30	fold	22	my	29	sun	16
bag	8	found	24	name	20	sunny	30
bake	20	from	26	neat	23	take	20
bat	6	fun	8	needed	34	ten	18
bath	32	funny	30	nest	9	they	29
being	35	game	20	not	17	this	15
big	15	gave	20	off	17	three	23
bike	21	glad	27	our	24	time	21
black	27	going	35	out	24	toad	22
blowing	35	got	17	passed	34	toe	22
blue	27	green	26	pay	29	top	12
book	12	grow	26	pen	9	train	26
both	22	hand	14	pig	8	trap	26
box	12	happy	30	pin	7	tree	23
broke	26	has	14	place	20	try	29
brown	26	hat	14	play	27	tub	6
bus	6	having	35	pony	30	us	6
but	16	heat	23	pop	12	van	11
came	20	hit	15	pulled	34	very	11
can	10	home	22	puppy	30	wanted	34
car	10	hook	7	queen	11	we	23
child	33	hop	7	red	18	went	18
chop	33	hot	7	rest	18	wet	10
clay	27	house	24	ride	21	when	32
clock	27	how	24	road	22	where	32
cold	10	hug	16	rope	22	white	32
cooked	34	jar	8	rowing	35	why	32
cry	29	jet	18	rug	10	will	10
day	29	job	17	run	16	win	15
den	9	jog	8	see	6	with	32
did	15	jump	16	she	33	you	11
dime	21	just	16	shoe	33	zip	11
dish	33	kite	21	shop	33	zoo	11
dog	9	lamp	14	show	33		
doing	35	last	28	singing	35		
down	24	leg	9	sit	6		
drink	26	like	21	six	12		
drop	17	looked	34	sky	29		
duck	9	lot	17	sleeping	35		
eat	23	lunch	33	slide	28		
end	18	make	20	slow	28		
fan	8	man	14	small	28		
father	32	many	30	snow	28		
feet	23	map	7	soap	22		
fill	15	meal	23	spoon	28		

All-Star Words

Word	Lesson
age	20
ax	12
bark	12
best	9
boat	6
bold	22
branch	33
bridge	26
carrying	35
cat	14
cent	18
chipmunk	33
clean	27
coat	22
cook	7
crossed	34
cub	6
cut	10
doe	22
drum	26
dry	29
family	30
fat	8
feather	32
fence	18
fish	15

Word	Lesson
flashlight	27
follow	17
food	8
fox	12
frown	24
froze	26
girl	8
glass	27
gray	29
great	26
grin	15
ground	24
hay	30
hiding	35
him	7
hunt	16
ice	21
joke	8
July	29
kick	15
ladybug	30
late	20
lock	17
log	9
luck	9
mask	14

Word	Lesson
maybe	29
men	9
milk	7
mud	16
neck	18
ouch	24
owl	24
paste	20
picked	34
pill	15
pipe	21
plane	27
played	34
pond	17
pot	17
pup	7
puppet	16
push	33
quick	11
ran	14
ringing	35
rock	10
seal	23
set	6
seven	18
she	23

Word	Lesson
should	33
sled	28
smile	21
speak	28
stand	14
step	12
stick	28
subway	30
summer	16
tadpole	22
tag	6
tame	20
teach	23
tooth	32
turned	34
vest	11
vine	21
wait	10
wall	10
watching	35
weed	23
west	28
wheel	32
whisper	32
yes	11
zebra	11

Spelling Enrichment

Bulletin-Board Suggestion

Doggone Good Spellers   Display large pictures of a doghouse, dog, and an empty food dish. Use tagboad to make dog bones. Encourage students to write any word on a bone that they are proud to be able to spell. Allow them to post as many bones as they wish onto the dog's dish each week.

You may also wish to display a chart listing students' names. Students can place checkmarks to keep track of the times they have posted bones onto the bulletin board. After a particular number of checkmarks, students can be awarded badges to wear to show they are good spellers. The badge might be a picture of a dog with the words "I'm a Doggone Good Speller."

Group Practice

Spinner   Write spelling words on index cards. Place the cards into six equal piles in front of the class. Number the piles 1 through 6. Then have the class line up into two teams. Using a game spinner that is numbered up to six, have students from opposing teams take turns spinning a number. The spinning player picks a word from the pile of the same number and hands it to an opponent. The opponent then reads the word while the player spells it. If the word is spelled correctly, the student who spinned may sit down and it is now the opponent's turn to spin. If the word is misspelled, the player continues to spin until a word is spelled correctly. The first team to be seated wins.

Fill-In   Write spelling words on the board. Omit some of the letters and replace them with dashes. Have the first student in Row One come to the board to fill in any of the missing letters in any of the words. Then have the first student in Row Two continue the procedure. Continue having students in each row take turns coming up to the board to fill in letters until all the words are completed. Any student who is able to correctly fill in a word earns a point for his row. The row with the most points at the end of the game wins.

Images   Distribute a sheet of drawing paper to each student. Encourage students to write or draw words in such a way that they form an image of the word's meaning. For example, the word "tall" may be drawn using tall letters. Likewise, words like "fat" or "huge" may be written using thick or balloon lettering. Words like "incline" or "hill" might be written so that they have an upward slant. You may want to have students refer to various spelling lessons for words that would work well with this activity.

Hidden Words   Choose a student to come up to the board to write a nonsense word. The nonsense word should be formed by combining two spelling words with one or more shared letters. The shared letters must end one word and begin the other. For example, the words "spot" and "they" can be joined to make the nonsense word "spothey." The student then calls on class members to identify and spell the two hidden words. The child who correctly identifies and spells the two words then gets to take a turn writing a new nonsense word on the board.

Erase   Write a word on the board. Then ask the class to put their heads down while you call on a student to come to the board and erase one or more of the letters in the word. This student then calls on a class member to identify the erased letter or letters. The student who correctly identifies the erasure can be the person who erases next.

Shape-Up   Prepare a set of large squares and rectangles made out of sturdy paper. Then divide the class into two teams. A student from Team One comes up to the chalk tray to arrange the squares and rectangles into a configuration of a List Word. (A configuration for the word "cat" would look like two squares joined to a vertical rectangle.) The student then whispers his or her word to the teacher. A student from Team Two must then write a List Word on the board that correctly matches the configuration. Although more than one word may match a configuration, a point is earned only when the written word matches the word whispered to the teacher. Whether a point is scored or not, the next member of Team Two now arranges a configuration for Team One to identify. Play continues in this manner until a configuration has been made for all the List Words.

Crossword Relay   First draw a large grid on the board. Then, divide the class into several teams. Teams compete against each other to form separate crossword puzzles on the board. Individuals on each team take turns racing against members of the other teams to join List Words until all possibilities have been exhausted. A List Word may appear on each crossword puzzle only once. The winning team is the team whose crossword puzzle contains the greatest number of correctly spelled List Words. In the case of a tie, the team finishing their puzzle first is the winner.

Scramble   Prepare letter cards sufficient to spell all the List Words. Distribute letter cards to all students. Some students may be given more than one letter card. The teacher then calls out a List Word. Students holding the letters contained in the word race to the front of the class to form the word by standing in the appropriate sequence with their letter cards.

Proofreading Relay   Write two columns of misspelled List Words on the board. Although the errors can differ, be sure that each list has the same number of errors. Divide the class into two teams and assign each team to a different column. Teams then compete against each other to correct their assigned lists by team members taking turns erasing and replacing an appropriate letter. Each member may correct only one letter per turn. The team that corrects its entire word list first wins.

Spelling Baseball   Using the board as home plate, designate other places in the classroom to be first, second, and third bases. Then divide the class into two teams. As the teacher pitches words from the spelling list, players in turn go to bat at writing the correct spelling of the word on the board. If the word is written correctly, the player can proceed to first base. The game continues in this manner with players advancing around the bases to score runs until an out is made by a player who misspells a word. The opposing team then takes its turn at bat.

Detective   Call on a student to be a detective. The detective must choose a spelling word from the list and think of a structural clue, definition, or synonym that will help classmates identify it. The detective then states the clue using the format, "I spy a word that . . . ." Students are called on to guess and spell the mystery word. Whoever answers correctly gets to take a turn being the detective.

Spelling Tic-Tac-Toe   Draw a tic-tac-toe square on the board. Divide the class into X and O teams. Take turns dictating spelling words to members of each team. If the word is spelled correctly, allow the team member to place an X or O on the square. The first team to place three X's or O's in a row wins.

Rhyming Roundup   Ask students to stand next to their desks. Then dictate pairs of words. Include words that are currently being studied. Ask students to clap their hands if they think the word pair rhymes. Students who clap their hands at inappropriate times should sit

down. See which students can remain standing for the longest time.

Spelldown   Teacher calls out a List Word as the first person in each row races to the board to write the beginning letter of the word. In turn, row members race to the board to continue spelling the word one letter at a time until the entire word is written. If a wrong letter is written, the next row member erases it and writes the correct letter. The first row to spell the entire word earns a point. Play continues in this manner until all the List Words have been dictated. The row with the most points wins the game and can be given a privilege, such as being first in line for recess or lunch.

Syllable Strips   Cut scrap paper into strips and distribute a bundle of strips to each student. Show students how to fold the paper into halves, thirds, and fourths. As the teacher pronounces a word for the class, students should fold a strip to correspond with the number of syllables heard in the word.

Word Guess   Set small balls of clay onto a smooth table at the front of the classroom. Call on a student to use clay to form the letters of a List Word. Then blindfold another student to guess what the word is by feeling the shape of the clay. Continue calling on different students to form the words and take guesses until all the List Words have been represented.

Words of Fortune   For this activity, a box of chips will be needed to use as tokens. Have students put their heads down while you write a spelling word on the board in large letters. Then cover each letter with a sheet of sturdy paper. The paper can be fastened to the board with magnets. Call on a student to guess any letter of the alphabet they think may be hidden. If that particular letter is hidden, then reveal the letter in every place where it appears in the word by removing the paper.

The student earns a token each time a letter is guessed correctly. The student continues to guess letters and earn tokens until an incorrect guess is made or the word is revealed. In the event that an incorrect guess is made, the student must return all tokens earned and a different student continues the game. Continue the game until every List Word has been hidden and then revealed. At the end of the game, allow students to trade tokens in for classroom privileges, such as being first in line. The amount of tokens needed to purchase each privilege may vary.

Spelling Enrichment

Dictionary Activities

Self-Correct Practice   As you dictate words from the list one at a time, have students write them. After each word is written, tell students to locate the word in their spelling dictionary. If they have written the word correctly, they can place a checkmark next to the word. If the word they have written is incorrect, have them copy the correct spelling from the dictionary and write it next to the word. Proceed in this manner until all the words have been dictated and corrected.

Around the World   Designate the first person in the first row to be the traveler. The traveler must stand next to the student seated behind him or her. Then dictate any letter of the alphabet at random. Instruct the two students to quickly name the letter of the alphabet that precedes the given letter. The student who is first to respond with the correct answer becomes the traveler while the other student sits at that desk. The traveler then moves to compete with the next person in the row. The game continues with the traveler moving up and down the rows as the teacher dictates various alphabet letters. See who can be the traveler who has moved the farthest around the classroom. For variety, the teacher may want at times to require students to state the letter that follows the given letter. You may also want to dictate pairs of List Words and have students name which word comes first.

Stand-Up   While the teacher pronounces a word from the spelling dictionary, students look up the entry word and point to it. Tell students to stand up when they have located the entry. See who is the first student to stand up.

This game can be played using the following variations:

1. Have students stand when they have located the guide words for a given word.

2. Have students stand when they are able to tell on what page a given List Word appears in the dictionary.

Alphabetical Scramble   Prepare tagboard cards with spelling words written on them in large letters. Distribute the cards to students. Call on three students to come to the front of the room and arrange themselves so that their word cards are in alphabetical order.

Cut-Off   Distribute a strip of paper to each student. Instruct students to write any four spelling words on the strip. All but one of the words should be in alphabetical order. Then have students exchange their strip with a partner. Students use scissors to cut off the word that is not in alphabetical sequence and tape the remaining word strips together. If students find this activity too difficult, you might have them cut all four words off the strip and arrange them alphabetically on their desks.

Applied Spelling

Journal   Allow time each day for students to write in a journal. A spiral bound notebook can be used for this purpose. Encourage students to express their feelings about events that are happening in their lives at home or at school. Or they could write about what their plans are for the day. To get them started, you may have to provide starter phrases. Allow them to use "invented" spelling for words they can't spell.

Collect the journals periodically to write comments that echo what the student has written. For example, a student's entry might read, "I'm hape I gt to plae bazball todae." The teacher's response could be, "Baseball is my favorite game, too. I'd be happy to watch you play baseball today at recess." This method allows students to learn correct spelling and sentence structure without emphasizing their errors in a negative way.

Letter to the Teacher   On a regular basis, invite students to write a note to you. At first you may have to suggest topics or provide a starter sentence. It may be possible to suggest a topic that includes words from the spelling list. Write a response at the bottom of each letter that provides the student with a model of any spelling or sentence structure that apparently needs improvement.

Daily Edit   Each day, provide a brief writing sample on the board that contains errors in spelling, capitalization, or punctuation. Have students rewrite the sample correctly. Provide time later in the day to have the class correct the errors on the board. Discuss why the spelling is as it is while students self-correct their papers.

Acrostic Poems   Have students write a word from the spelling list vertically. Then instruct them to join a word horizontally to each letter of the List Word. The horizontal words must begin with the letters in the List

Word. They also should be words that describe or relate feelings about the List Word. Encourage students to refer to a dictionary for help in finding appropriate words. Here is a sample acrostic poem:

Zebras
Otters
Ostriches

Words-in-a-Row   Distribute strips of writing paper to each student. Ask students to write three spelling words in a row. Tell them to misspell two of the words. Then have students take turns writing their row of words on the board. They can call on a classmate to identify and underline the correctly spelled word in the row. Continue until all students have had a chance to write their row of words.

Nursery Rhyme Exchange   Provide students with copies of a familiar nursery rhyme. Discuss how some of the words can be exchanged for other words that have similar meanings. Ask students to rewrite the nursery rhyme exchanging some of the words. You may want to encourage students to try this technique with nursery rhymes of their choice. Be sure to give students the opportunity to read their rhymes to the class.

Story Starters   From time to time the teacher may find that some of the spelling lessons contain words that suggest an idea for a story. Feel free to use your creativity to provide students with a good starter sentence or suggestion for a story, but do not require students to use words from the spelling list. Let them generate their own story vocabulary. Story starters should stimulate creative thinking. For example: "Imagine you have just swallowed a shrinking pill. What is happening around you?"

Partner Spelling   Assign spelling buddies. Allow partners to alternate dictating or writing sentences that contain words from the spelling list. The sentences can be provided by the teacher or generated by students. Have students check their own work as their partner provides the correct spelling for each sentence.

Scrap Words   Provide each student with several sheets of tagboard, scraps of fabric or wallpaper, and some glue. Ask students to cut letters out of the scrap materials and glue them to the tagboard to form words from the spelling list. Display the colorful scrap words around the classroom.

Punch Words   Set up a work center in the classroom with a supply of construction paper strips, a hole puncher, sheets of thin paper, and crayons. Demonstrate to students how the hole puncher can be used to create spelling words out of the construction paper. Permit students to take turns working at the center in their free time. Students may also enjoy placing a thin sheet of paper over the punch words and rubbing them with a crayon to make colorful word designs. You can then display their punch word and crayon creations.

Word Cut-Outs   Distribute scissors, glue, a sheet of dark-colored construction paper, and a supply of old newspapers and magazines to the class. Have students look through the papers and magazines for spelling List Words. Tell them to cut out any List Words they find and glue them onto the sheet of construction paper. See who can find the most spelling List Words. This technique may also be used to have students construct sentences.

Word Sorts   Invite students to write each List Word on a separate card. Then ask them how many different ways the words can be organized (e.g., animate vs. inanimate, similarity or contrast in meaning, vowel or consonant patterns). As students sort the words into each category, have them put words that don't belong in a category into an exception pile.

Definitions and Rules

The alphabet has two kinds of letters. The **vowels** are **a, e, i, o,** and **u** (and sometimes **y** and **w**). All the rest of the letters are **consonants.**

Each **syllable** in a word must have a vowel sound. If a word or syllable has only one vowel and it comes at the beginning or between two consonants, the vowel usually stands for a **short** sound.

cat   sit   cup

A **long-vowel** sound usually has the same sound as its letter name.

When **y** comes at the end of a word with one syllable, the **y** at the end spells /ī/, as in dry and try. When **y** comes at the end of a word with more than one syllable, it usually has the sound of /ē/, as in city and funny.

When two or more **consonants** come together in a word, their sounds may blend together. In a **consonant blend,** you can hear the sound of each letter.

smile   **sl**ide   **fr**iend

A **consonant digraph** consists of two consonants that go together to make one sound.

sharp   four**th**   ea**ch**

A **consonant cluster** is three consonants together in one syllable.

thrills   pa**tch**   **spl**ash

A **suffix** is an addition made at the **end** of a **root word.**

rain**ed**   help**ed**

A **prefix** is a word part that is added to the beginning of another word called a **root word.** A prefix changes the meaning of the root.

unhappy   **dis**trust

When you write words in **alphabetical order,** use these rules:

1. If the first letter of two words is the same, use the second letter.

2. If the first two letters are the same, use the third letter.

There are two **guide words** at the top of each page in the dictionary. The word on the left tells you the first word on the page. The word on the right tells you the last word on the page. All the words in between are in **alphabetical order.**

The dictionary puts an **accent mark** (´) after the syllable with the strong sound.

per´son

There is a vowel sound that can be spelled by any of the vowels. It is often found in a syllable that is *not accented,* or stressed, in a word. This vowel sound has the sound-symbol /ə/. It is called the **schwa.**

The word I is always a **capital** letter.

A **contraction** is a short way of writing two words. It is formed by writing two words together and leaving out one or more letters. Use an **apostrophe** (') to show where something is left out.

it is = it's   we will = we'll

A **compound word** is a word made by joining two or more words.

cannot   anyway   maybe

Teacher's Notes